DEALING

OTHER BOOKS BY TERRY PLUTO

ON SPORTS:
False Start: How the New Browns Were Set Up to Fail
The View from Pluto
Unguarded (with Lenny Wilkens)
Our Tribe
Browns Town 1964
Burying the Curse
The Curse of Rocky Colavito
Falling from Grace
Tall Tales
Loose Balls
Bull Session (with Johnny Kerr)
Tark (with Jerry Tarkanian)
Forty-Eight Minutes, a Night in the Life of the NBA (with Bob Ryan)
Sixty-One (with Tony Kubek)
You Could Argue But You'd Be Wrong (with Pete Franklin)
Weaver on Strategy (with Earl Weaver)
The Earl of Baltimore
Super Joe (with Joe Charboneau and Burt Graeff)
The Greatest Summer

ON FAITH AND OTHER TOPICS:
Faith and You
Everyday Faith
Champions for Life: The Power of a Father's Blessing (with Bill Glass)
Crime: Our Second Vietnam (with Bill Glass)

DEALING

The Cleveland Indians' New Ballgame:
Inside the Front Office and the Process
of Rebuilding a Contender

TERRY PLUTO

GRAY & COMPANY, PUBLISHERS
CLEVELAND

© 2006 by Terry Pluto

All rights reserved. No part of this book may be reproduced
or transmitted in any form or manner without written
permission from the publisher, except in the case of brief
quotations embodied in critical articles and reviews.

Gray & Company, Publishers
www.grayco.com

Library of Congress Cataloging-in-Publication Data
Pluto, Terry, 1955-
Dealing: the Cleveland Indians' new ballgame: inside the
front office and the process of rebuilding a contender /
Terry Pluto.
p. cm.
1. Cleveland Indians (Baseball team)—History. 2. Cleveland Indians (Baseball team)—Management. 3. Cleveland
Indians (Baseball team)—Finance. I. Title.
GV875.C7P584 2006
796.357'640977132—dc22   2006010683

ISBN-13: 978-1-59851-022-5
ISBN-10: 1-59851-022-3

Printed in the United States of America
First printing

To the memory of my father, Tom Pluto
He gave me two great gifts: His love for me
and a love for the Cleveland Indians.

CONTENTS

———

DEALING

"NO ONE KNEW WHAT WAS COMING."

FACING A SCARY NEW BALLGAME

The Cleveland Indians were supposed to keep ruling the American League's Central Division forever. Fans came to believe that during those heady Indian summers of the middle and late 1990s. Regular trips to the playoffs, steady sellouts at Jacobs Field, a team with one of baseball's ten highest payrolls . . . Who didn't think the glory days would continue, at least for another decade?

Most fans did. And so did Mark Shapiro.

Shapiro became the Indians' general manager after the 2001 season. He inherited a talent-filled team with a $96 million payroll, third highest in baseball. On his desk were five-year projections showing payrolls between $80 million and $100 million. It wasn't New York Yankees money, but it sure wasn't a bargain-basement Tampa Bay budget, either.

Yet there was trouble ahead.

"No one knew what was coming," said Shapiro.

By the end of the 2001 season, the Indians and their fans were faced with a whole new ballgame. Fans still had high expectations, but the front office no longer had a budget to match. The veteran team was aging quickly. The long string of sellouts had ended, and sales of luxury suites and loges slowed. The future no longer looked certain. If anything, it was scary.

It had been just two years since the Dolan family bought the team from Dick Jacobs, and "there were major cracks in the foundation," according to Shapiro.

The team's baseball operations had problems, from the weakened scouting staff to the neglected farm system to the overpaid and underproducing big league roster. The local economy had suddenly gone bad, then gotten worse. Jacobs Field was no longer a novelty, nor was a winning baseball team. The Cleveland Browns were back, and despite their dismal expansion-era record Cleveland remains a football town. The Browns sold out every game. The arrival of LeBron James had made the NBA's Cavaliers a hot ticket. The Indians, meanwhile, now had lots of good seats available nearly every game.

"Everything that converged in the 1990s to make that bubble where we had some payrolls in the top five in baseball—all those things were gone," said Shapiro. "I knew that. But no one knew how low revenues would go, or how much the attendance would drop. No one ever thought we'd be in the bottom five of payrolls. I mean nobody."

Maybe a few people did.

Dick Jacobs had a clue. That's why he sold the team after the 1999 season to the Dolan family. Perhaps the former Tribe owner didn't know how far the team would fall in terms of attendance and payroll, but he knew there would little growth. He also knew stars such as Manny Ramirez would soon be leaving as free agents.

Former Indians GM John Hart also sensed something. About six months after Jacobs sold the team to the Dolan family in 2000, Hart confided to Shapiro (then his assistant) that 2001 would be his last year—and he wanted Shapiro to take his place as general manager.

"John talked to me like a friend," said Shapiro. "He said he was going to Larry and Paul Dolan with a succession plan in mind, which is common in business but rare in baseball. He said he was ready to do something different. He didn't say what. We talked about what the next few years would bring. But we had no idea what really was coming."

Tough times were coming.

The Indians went from winning the Central Division in 2001 with 91 wins to losing 94 games in 2003.

The Indians went from a $96 million payroll in 2001 to payrolls in the $40 million range starting in 2003 and continuing the next few years.

The Indians went from sellout crowds to playing in front of a small circle of family and friends some weeknights.

"We had to learn a new way to deal with this," said Shapiro.

If the Indians' new reality began when the Dolan family purchased the team from Dick Jacobs, it came into sharper focus with the departure of John Hart.

Hart had been general manager since 1992. He combined with manager Mike Hargrove to win five Central Division titles and make two trips to the World Series. After the 1999 season, Hart knew it was over. But he would never say that. Instead, he hoped he could keep the Indians in the playoffs, squeeze out one more trip to the World Series.

Because, as Hart liked to say, "Once you're in the playoffs, who knows what will happen?"

Like in 1997, when the Indians won only 86 games, but were the surprise of baseball by coming within a single pitch of winning the World Series, eventually losing the Seventh Game to the Florida Marlins.

By 1999, though, Hart had to know something had changed. The Indians had an impressive 97–65 record, winning the Central Division by 22 games. They should have been confident heading into the playoffs.

"But there was an uneasiness, a lot of pressure on Mike [Hargrove] to win or else," recalled veteran Tribe broadcaster Tom Hamilton. "I'd seen this building up for a number of years. No matter what we did in the regular season, it wasn't good enough for anybody. We still were entertaining, but fans took the playoffs for granted. Instead of excitement, there was this sense of uncertainty, 'What if we don't win?' Most of us sensed, if we didn't have a good October, a change would be made."

(Hamilton's insights are important because he is more than just the team's respected radio broadcaster; he is often taken into confidence by the front office about team policy. His advice is not sought, but the Indians want him to know what they are doing and why they are doing it. He also is close to many of the players and coaches.)

That 1999 team was limping in the playoffs. History tells us that it was a tired, seemingly stale group of players.

"I don't see it quite like that," said Hargrove. "We just had some injuries at the wrong time. [Dave] Burba's arm was hurting. So was Mike Jackson's. There were some other guys who were kind of physically beat up. [Travis] Fryman's back was bothering him. It's just like the momentum turned on us."

The Indians won the first two games of the best-of-five Division Series with Boston, but then lost the next three by a combined score of 45–18. A desperate Hargrove juggled his pitching rotation to counteract the injuries, starting Bartolo Colon and Charles Nagy in the final two games of the series on three days' rest, instead of their usual four. Both pitchers were hit hard. It seemed nothing worked for Hargrove. It appeared that all the goodwill built up by the team over the 1990s evaporated when a sore-armed Pedro Martinez strutted in from the bullpen and shut down the Indians with sheer will and a mediocre fastball, the Tribe showing itself to be an uptight team that no longer believed in itself. That Indians' season ended with one of the greatest collapses in playoff history. Hargrove immediately took the fall, fired by Hart at the end of the season.

To this day, Hargrove finds it difficult to discuss, other than to say, "It wasn't fair. I felt betrayed."

Hart and Hargrove had their private and public battles, but they formed a remarkable team that survived nearly nine years. That's a couple of lifetimes in baseball, where the average manager's tenure is about three years. They won a lot of games. They inspired confidence in most fans. They put together some of the best teams in Tribe history. But that baseball marriage wasn't the only thing that ended after the 1999 playoffs. So did the Indians as a legitimate American League pennant contender, although no one was ready to face that painful truth. By firing Hargrove and promoting hitting coach Charlie Manuel to take his place, Hart was falling into an old baseball ploy that rarely works in the long haul—changing the manager. If the guy you just fired had a 97–65 record and won the division by 21 games, what is the next manager supposed to do?

At the press conference where Manuel's promotion was announced, Hart talked about "going to the next level."

All that remained was winning the World Series.

But a hard look at the Tribe roster, combined with a serious analysis of the suddenly failing scouting and farm system in the late 1990s, revealed the patient had an irregular heartbeat. The arteries were starting to clog. The body parts just didn't function as well as they once had. A quick fix like switching managers was not even close to the miracle cure this patient needed.

"I remember seeing a highly paid Mets team a few years ago," said Tribe vice president Bob DiBiasio. "They came to Jacobs Field and looked totally disinterested. They sleepwalked through three games. I realized that was how we looked at times [in 1999]. It led to John Hart changing managers."

What the Indians really needed to do after 1999 was begin to seriously change players, and not just bring in one recycled veteran to replace another.

"We couldn't go in that direction," said DiBiasio. "Even though we had times when we were a veteran, disinterested team, we were still talented. We could still get to the playoffs."

There was another reason: money.

After the 1999 playoffs, the Dolans paid $320 million for the Tribe, at the time the highest price ever paid for a major league franchise. Their fans were used to winning. The Dolans had to promise even more winning. And to win now, they had to pay now. So the payroll was high.

"The flaws did begin to be revealed in that playoff," said Indians president Paul Dolan. "We collapsed in Game Four, then again in Game Five. We began to realize that we could not sustain this as it presently was put together. I saw we were getting older. I knew we had to get younger, but we couldn't just turn the team upside down and keep our credibility."

Instead, the Dolans kept spending in 2000 and 2001. They signed ancient and expensive free agents such as Chuck Finley and Ellis Burks. They bought a $14 million baseball lottery ticket on Cuban import Danys Baez, a pitcher not as polished as advertised. They took over a team with a $72 million payroll in 1999 and raised it to $82 million in 2000, then $96 million in 2001.

They were spending like no Tribe owners ever had before. According to Paul Dolan, they dug a $30 million hole of debt after those first two seasons that yielded a grand total of one playoff appearance, a first-round elimination to Seattle.

It was over, but no one wanted to admit it. Not the front office. Not the media. Not the fans. The patient needed heart surgery, but John Hart didn't want to operate. Not again. Not when he knew that all he'd get was criticism. Not when he also knew it might not work. Not when he believed that by the late 1990s, fan and media expectations were out of control, and few people truly appreciated what had been accomplished in the those years.

John Hart often said it was so much more fun to build a team than to try and maintain one. He said he found himself making trades he knew could explode in his face because he believed he had to win now. He sensed he was in a no-win situation. If the Indians did somehow get back to the World Series, well, that was expected. If not, it was his fault for not coming up with the talent.

Hart had discussed all this with Shapiro.

"The prospect of going through another painful transition with a passionate fan base that had high standards was something he could handle, but at that stage of his career, it wasn't something he wanted to do," said Shapiro. "John was good enough and worked hard enough to make his own call, rather than have it made for him. He made his own call [to leave]. He knew it was going to be different with the Dolans now owning the team, but he never in a million years thought it would be what it's like now. None of us did. There are times when I feel like I can't make a mistake, like there is no margin for error with our payroll. Any significant player move has to turn out right because we don't have the budget like some other teams. There's no eraser."

That's the reality of Cleveland Indians baseball.

From the last pitch of the 2001 playoffs, when the Indians lost in Seattle, Shapiro realized he needed a new and daring plan. The fans might not like it. It might not work. It could even cost him a chance to ever be a general manager again. But clearly things had to change.

This is a story of dealing, from the owner's box to the front office to the dugout. It's about how the people running the Cleveland Indians franchise realized they were confronted with a new baseball reality and would have to . . .

Deal with a Central Division that was no longer the Tribe's personal playpen.

Deal with a fan base that had become a bit spoiled, no longer content just to make the playoffs but anxious to win Cleveland's first World Series since 1948.

Deal with declining season ticket sales and corporate sponsorship.

Deal with fans and media still angry about losing stars such as Jim Thome, Manny Ramirez and Bartolo Colon.

Deal with the fact that many of those who helped set attendance records in the 1990s were not hardcore baseball disciples. They were attracted by the winning and the glitz of the new Jacobs Field.

Deal with the Dolan family finances, which had taken a hit of about $30 million in 2000 and 2001, and couldn't be stretched further.

Deal with an outgrown payroll by trading big names for young players with no names in the hope of rebuilding a winner on a tighter budget . . .

Five years later, as the 2006 season approached, Shapiro still sounded a little stunned when talking about the dramatic changes in the franchise. The plummeting payroll. (The New York Yankees were now spending five times as much on players as the Tribe.) The dwindling attendance. (The Indians struggled to draw slightly more than 2 million in 2005; in the American League, only Kansas City and Detroit attracted fewer.)

Yet his bold moves seemed to be working on the field.

The Indians were once again in contention, winning 93 games in 2005 and falling just one game short of a return trip to the playoffs. Shapiro was named Major League Baseball's 2005 Executive of the Year after the Indians won those 93 games with a $45 million payroll, which ranked in baseball's bottom five. The core of an exciting young team was beginning to take shape. In just three years, Shapiro had given the Indians a heart transplant—along with replacing nearly every other major body part along the way.

To understand how successful the surgery was, you should understand how the Indians found themselves in such desperate condition in the first place.

CHAPTER 1

"IS THIS TEAM FOR SALE?"

DICK JACOBS BUYS LOW, SELLS HIGH

He always wanted to get there first.

Remember that about Dick Jacobs.

He always believed in buying low, selling high.

Remember that about Dick Jacobs, too.

Those attributes explain why Jacobs bought the Indians after the 1986 season, and why he put them up for sale during the 1999 season, eventually cutting a deal with the Dolan family that led to a sale approved on January 19, 2000.

Jacobs bought *very* low, sold *very* high.

In between, he pulled off some very shrewd moves. He convinced the county to build Jacobs Field, which became one of the game's new breed of cash-cow stadiums, gushing profits for Jacobs. Then he took the team to Wall Street, putting together a public stock offering that, over eighteen months, paid a 50 percent return to its investors, the biggest of whom was Dick Jacobs. No other Major League Baseball franchise had ever sold shares like this before.

In between, the Indians had their best run in franchise history.

Start with a story Jacobs told me before the 1995 season. I was asking him about business, how much money he'd make that year, how much he lost at the old stadium, the financial health of the franchise. He declined to talk recent profits, though he mentioned about $40 million in losses from 1987 to 1993. Instead, he talked about Swenson's, an Akron hamburger joint, a drive-in with real carhops, still around, still a local legend.

Jacobs grew up in the Goodyear Heights section of Akron, where he said you could smell burning rubber from the plant where his father worked. By the time he was ten years old, Jacobs was mowing lawns for nickels and dimes. This was during the Depression. One of his customers was Wes Swenson, owner of the hamburger joint. It took two years, but Jacobs convinced Swenson to hire him. First, he peeled potatoes in the kitchen, but his eye was on the parking lot. That's where the real action was, where carhops rushed to customers, took orders through the window, then ran back to the kitchen. When the food was ready, the carhops sprinted it back to the customer. It was all about looking sharp, serving quick, grabbing as many tips as possible.

"You wanted to get to the right cars first," he told me. "After a year in the kitchen, I was a carhop. I could spot a Caddy coming two blocks away. I got my big foot out there first and told the other guys 'That one is mine.' I figured out which cars had the best tippers, and I made sure they were the ones that I waited on."

Jacobs likes to talk about mowing lawns, peeling potatoes, serving burgers. He says little about the real estate deals that had made his company worth about $500 million by 1986, when he and his brother David made their move to buy the Indians. At the time, Jacobs owned forty-two malls and eighteen Wendy's restaurants in the Columbus area. He also had some hotels in places such as Key West, where he was part of that Florida city's real estate explosion. He had developed and sold countless shopping centers and malls over the previous decades. He was one of the first to figure out that America's move from the city to the suburbs meant more than the need for housing. These people needed a place to shop, and they no longer wanted to drive or take the bus downtown. So he started with strip shopping centers in the suburbs, then switched to indoor malls. He realized malls had become the new gathering centers, much like the old town halls.

By the time he was negotiating for the Indians in 1986, Jacobs had seen a new opportunity. Now, downtown areas—and Cleveland in particular—were poised for a revival. He believed if a new ballpark could be built downtown, not only would it save the Indians for Cleveland, it could save Cleveland as a viable city, open for business. It could be a magnet for other businesses. It could inspire some confidence in other businessmen and investors. And, of course, it could make him a lot of money.

This could be his biggest deal yet, not because of the money, but because so many people would be watching.

What Jacobs was watching was a seemingly comatose baseball team owned by a dead man. For two years, the Indians had been in the estate of Steve O'Neill. His nephew, Pat O'Neill, had been put in charge of finding a buyer. The Indians were losers, on the field and at the bank. They needed a new stadium, but it appeared it would be years—maybe decades—before that would happen. There were legitimate fears the franchise would move to another city.

I developed a relationship with Pat O'Neill because we had both attended Cleveland Benedictine High School. Even though I was covering the Cleveland Cavaliers and NBA basketball at the time for the *Akron Beacon Journal*, he called me the night of the sale to give me the only interview about the deal he'd just made. He told me the new owners of the Indians were two brothers named David and Dick Jacobs, who developed shopping malls.

I'd never heard of them. No one even knew they were talking to O'Neill.

"These are great guys," O'Neill told me. "Dick came in and his words were, 'Is this team for sale?' No messing around."

Jacobs asked that question because Pat O'Neill had been unable to find a buyer for two years, and there was some thought that he might try to hold onto the team for a while. Jacobs explained why he and his brother wanted the Indians, how they planned to work with the politicians to lobby for the building of a new stadium. He stressed they were Cleveland guys, heavily invested in local real estate. It would be public relations suicide for them to move the team, a real possibility with many of the buyers approaching O'Neill. Then Jacobs explained that they had some cash and a viable way to make the sale work.

"The first time I talked to Dick, I knew that he and his brother were the guys," Pat O'Neill told me that night. "They're our kind of people, old school. Clevelanders. They'll keep the team here."

O'Neill believed Dick and Dave Jacobs could find a way to make a deal for a new stadium because they had built so many huge shopping malls and office buildings. Unlike some other bidders who talked so much but had so little of anything tangible to show, the Jacobs brothers kept their words to a whispered minimum. But their financial empire screamed that these were men of action. Dick Jacobs did most of the negotiating. David was more of a silent partner. (David Jacobs died in 1992, which is why few fans even remember he was part of the original sale.)

They cut a deal to buy the Indians that broke down like this:

- About $18 million in cash
- About $3 million in a loan from the O'Neill estate
- About $14 million in loans from different banks, which they inherited from the previous ownership

"Part of the reason we bought it was I didn't want the Indians to end up in St. Petersburg or somewhere else," Jacobs once told me. "In the past, some of the owners didn't have the money to run the team. Others had it, but didn't feel comfortable making the investment."

Jacobs was prepared to invest more in his new team, but he would do it on his own schedule. In his first year, the Indians lost 101 games. They drew slightly more than 1 million fans. The farm system was a mess, and so was scouting. This was clearly a long-term project, and he was in it for the long haul.

Jacobs knew that buying a property at the right time was only part of the deal. You also had to put the right people in charge of it. He brought in veteran baseball man Hank Peters to run the Indians in the late 1980s with the goal of building a team. Peters would create a productive farm system while slashing the major league payroll to pay for it. He also was ready to make tough trades, such as dealing Joe Carter, one of the team's only stars, for minor league prospects Carlos Baerga and Sandy Alomar. Peters also was to train a new general manager to eventually take his place. Then when the Indians were ready to contend, Peters knew, he'd be retired. But he was a good-soldier executive, willing to dirty his hands digging the foundation even though he'd never get to live in the mansion.

Peters had done a stint with the Indians as minor league director before serving as the Baltimore Orioles' general manager in the 1970s and early 1980s. Jacobs admired the Orioles, and when Peters had a problem with free-agent-obsessed owner Peter Angelos, Jacobs stepped in and hired Peters. That was important to Peters, who was discouraged in his final years with Baltimore: Jacobs made him feel wanted. And everyone said Jacobs could be trusted. So Peters went to work, and it was Peters who hired an obscure minor league manager named John Hart with the intention of making Hart the Tribe's next general manager.

Jacobs didn't know Hart, but he trusted Peters. It was Peters who trained John Hart to become general manager. It was Hart and his assistant, Dan O'Dowd, who convinced Jacobs to sign young players to long-term deals in the early 1990s, keeping them away from free agency longer. It was Jacobs who stayed patient.

"I had been a general manager for less than a year, and I was asking my owner to commit millions of dollars to a plan that had never been done before," Hart told me in 1995.

It was 1992. Hart was coming off an arbitration case involving Indians starting pitcher Greg Swindell, who was 12–9 with a 4.40 ERA in 1991. Swindell won a $2 million salary, putting him among the most highly paid 10 percent of all pitchers in baseball. Hart was disappointed with the results and told O'Dowd, "The arbitrator is not even a baseball guy. We are never going to go through this again."

O'Dowd, a man who loves ideas and is willing to take chances, in many ways reflected Hart. While the two of them were twenty-five thousand feet above the ground, sitting next to each other in an airplane, they decided to put their heads in the clouds and adopt a new approach.

"We were trying to save a doomed franchise," Hart recalled. "Big-market teams were going to just blow us out of the water. We'd continue to lose our best and brightest young players— either to free agency, or be forced to trade them before they became free agents."

That's when O'Dowd and Hart concocted a plan to sign their best young players, such as second baseman Carlos Baerga, catcher Sandy Alomar, pitcher Charles Nagy, and others, to long-term deals after their first season or two in the big leagues. Early in their careers, it seemed these players would be overpaid. They also would have financial security that they had yet to earn. But these multiyear contracts would help the team project its future for the next three years.

"I've never been afraid to take risks," Jacobs told me in 1995. "John had his honor on the line, I had my checkbook."

"If it hadn't worked, I'd never be a general manager again," Hart said. "I had other general managers calling me, asking me what was I doing. What if these guys got hurt? What if they couldn't play?"

They signed eleven players. Not all became stars. Long forgotten are the multiyear deals given to Mark Whiten, Jack Armstrong, Scott Scudder, Dave Otto, and Glenallen Hill. But there were more hits than misses, from Baerga to Alomar to Nagy to Albert Belle. Then, just when all this young talent began to mature, Jacobs put out $14 million to sign veterans Dennis Martinez and Eddie Murray for the 1994 season. They played a key role in the 1995 pennant-winning team, as did another veteran free agent, Orel Hershiser, signed before the 1995 season.

"That was expensive," Jacobs said of signing the free agents. "But I wanted the success and character from those guys to rub off on our young players. We also were moving into Jacobs Field, and I could make some projections on our revenue. That made it easier to move forward."

Jacobs Field was the key piece.

No ballpark, no contender.

Maybe no Cleveland Indians.

Jacobs worked with the Cleveland and Cuyahoga County political powers to get the new Gateway development project moving, with a baseball park at its center. He had no interest in Cleveland Browns owner Art Modell's plans to renovate the old Cleveland Stadium.

Modell wanted to hang on to the Stadium. He had been renting it from the city for years for a token amount. He had poured millions into the sagging structure and wanted to recoup some of that investment.

The last thing Jacobs wanted was Modell as a landlord.

"It's hard for two guys to share the same lunch box," Jacobs told me years later.

Especially if one of the guys was Art Modell. Jacobs would never have said so, but it was obvious that he, like most other members of Cleveland's millionaire business community, knew Modell had financial problems.

Jacobs wanted to control his own facility. He realized that a new ballpark in the heart of the city, not on the lakefront, was needed to wipe away some of the blight and begin the healing of downtown Cleveland.

Modell didn't jump immediately into the Gateway project. He was still trying to save his own stadium, and was not thrilled that Jacobs had no interest in his banged-up lunch box on Lake Erie.

Jacobs kept moving forward, and Modell was left behind on the stadium issue.

The Gateway project delivered Jacobs Field and Gund Arena, the new home of the Cleveland Cavaliers. Owner Gordon Gund had been recruited to bring the Cavaliers from the suburban Richfield Coliseum to downtown in order to help convince Cuyahoga County voters to approve a countywide tax on tobacco and alcohol. The levy passed. Jacobs Field was built. The Indians moved in for the 1994 season and became immediate contenders.

From 1994 to 1999, the Indians were exactly what Jacobs said he wanted them to be during interviews in the early 1990s: "I want a contender with a positive cash flow and a fair return on our investment."

"With Dick Jacobs, when he was set on something, that usually was it. End of discussion," said Ken Stefanov, the Tribe's senior vice president of finance and chief financial officer. "Mr. Jacobs loved going to games. He was proud of what the team did and of being owner of the Indians. He'd often say, 'This was fun.' But he also wanted us to run at a profit."

The rise of the team and the new ballpark created a gold mine for Jacobs. But you also have to give the owner credit for staying with Hank Peters and John Hart in the long, losing years before the Jacobs Field era. And give Jacobs credit for not trying to tell his baseball people how to do their business. He set a budget, but Jacobs didn't demand that the general manager trade for a certain third baseman because he had happened to see the guy have a good game on TV. He was not influenced by public opinion, either from the fans or media.

"Mr. Jacobs was a great owner to work for," said Mike Hargrove, the Tribe's manager from 1991 to 1999. "We'd meet with him. He was interested in what we wanted to do and wanted to hear the reasons. But I'm telling you, he was supportive. He respected John [Hart] and I. He let us do our jobs. We knew he was behind us. He liked stability. I have the utmost respect for him."

Hargrove said this in a January 2006 interview. He talked about how Jacobs was able to make sure that everyone left a meeting heading in the same direction. He believes that Jacobs's steady hand was a key to the Indians' success. While other teams continually changed the front office and field managers, Jacobs insisted everyone work together.

"If you have a good plan and just stick with it and the key people behind it, you're going to come out all right," said Hargrove. "That's what we did."

Jacobs owned the team from 1987 to 1999. He had two general managers, Hart and Peters. After shuffling through managers Doc Edwards, John McNamara, and even Hart (briefly), the Indians settled on Hargrove as skipper at the All-Star break of 1991. Hargrove and others believe that Hart was close to firing him in July of 1997, and perhaps during another season, but Jacobs demanded that everyone just wait. Hargrove survived. In 1997, the Indians went to the World Series. Hargrove was fired after the 1999 season, but Jacobs was in the process of finalizing the sale to the Dolan family and out of the daily decision-making process.

If you look at the numbers, you begin to figure out why Dick Jacobs sold the team when he did. Especially when you consider that Dick Jacobs never intended to make this a family business. (It's doubtful that he viewed any investment as permanent.) In 1995, he made $6.7 million with the Indians. It would have been more, but because of the baseball strike at the start of the season, the Indians played only 144 games instead of 162, missing out on 18 games.

These and other numbers became public when Jacobs decided to put the Indians stock on the open market in 1998. He was following the lead of the NBA's Boston Celtics, who did it in 1986 to raise cash. (The owners guessed—correctly—that fans would buy small portions of stock as souvenirs.)

Here's what the stock prospectus revealed:

1993: $3.9 million profit (Last year at the old Cleveland Stadium. Included $3 million share of expansion fees from Colorado and Florida)
1994: $500,000 loss because of the baseball strike
1995: $6.7 million profit
1996: $10.2 million profit
1997: $22.6 million profit
1998: $13.9 million profit

It's a reasonable guess that Jacobs made a profit in the $7 million range in 1999, his final year owning the franchise. That season is not part of the public record.

According to Tribe records, the team's major league player payroll rose from $18 million in 1993 to $61 million in 1997. For the 1998 season, Jacobs paid himself a $700,000 salary. Hart earned $600,000. Dan O'Dowd, the assistant general manager, and Dennis Lehman, executive vice president of business, each drew a $300,000 salary.

Appearing in the postseason also paid off, as the profits from the 1995 to 1998 postseason appearances show:

Year	Profit	Games	Result
1995	$4.4 million	15 (8 home)	Lost to Atlanta, 6-game World Series
1996	$624,000	4 (2 home)	Lost to Baltimore, 1st round
1997	$6.8 million	18 (9 home)	Lost to Florida, 7-game World Series
1998	$5.4 million	10 (5 home)	Lost to Yankees, 2nd round

The Jacobs Field deal was also very, very favorable to the owner. Here's the rent paid from 1994 to 1997:

1994: $102,537 paid. The team would pay no rent if it failed to draw at least 1.85 million fans. The announced attendance was 1.99 million.

1995: $1.3 million paid.

1996: $1.6 million paid.

1997: $2.1 million paid.

1998: $1.9 million paid.

1999: $1.8 million paid.

"The 455-game sellout streak [from June 12, 1995, to April 4, 2001] was remarkable," said Stefanov, the Indians' vice president of finance. "But even more amazing was our no-show rate during that time. It was about 9 percent, the lowest in baseball. For example, in 2003 and 2004 it was about 20 percent."

That's important, because fans who buy tickets but don't attend the games do more than make the stadium look empty. They are also *not* buying hot dogs, drinks, caps, and bobbleheads.

"We estimate that each fan spends about seven dollars to ten dollars [per person] in food and beverages, another two to three dollars in merchandise," said Stefanov.

Suppose you sell 40,000 tickets for game, and 10 percent fail to show—that's 4,000. By Stefanov's math, the team loses about $45,000 in food and merchandise revenue. But if 20 percent—or 8,000—don't show, then it's $90,000 per game.

You can be sure that Jacobs understood these numbers, too.

After the Indians had the heartbreaking loss to Florida in the 1997 World Series, it's possible Jacobs began to realize he couldn't sell any more tickets or any more commercial time for his media outlets than were already being sold. It was hard to imagine selling many more caps, jackets, and shirts. Yet his payroll was going up. That's when he decided to take the team to Wall Street and sell stock.

Jacobs, along with team vice presidents Dennis Lehman, Stefanov, and Hart made stops at several large investment firms to stir interest in the stock. Jacobs told me how he hated being questioned and sometimes lectured by brokers and investment experts who were so young they could be his grandchildren. He is not a man who likes to explain business, he just does business.

Jacobs had a plan.

Get in, get out.

He never told anyone that. He probably would not admit as much today.

But less than a year after selling shares in the Indians, he put the team up for sale, and six months later the deal with the Dolan family was set. The stock that originally sold for $15 and dropped as low as $6 eventually was worth $22 when Jacobs sold out.

That's a 50 percent profit in eighteen months for the investors.

Not long after the shares became available, a team official asked me if I had bought some. I explained how it paid no dividends and seemed to have no real chance to make a profit. The executive agreed, but then said, "I have no inside information whatsoever. But you and I know Dick Jacobs. You know the man makes money. You know this is going to make him a lot of money, even if we don't know how right now. I'm buying."

I should have done the same thing, but didn't.

Some baseball executives estimate that Jacobs walked away with about $60 million from the stock deal.

There was another factor behind Jacobs's decision to sell: he knew what was coming, and he didn't want to be a part of it.

Jacobs met occasionally with friends such as former Cavaliers general manager Wayne Embry, with whom he would discuss the economics of baseball. Unlike football and basketball, baseball was unable to install any type of salary cap. Jacobs saw Indians slugger Albert Belle turn down $40 million for five years after the 1996 season, signing with the White Sox for $55 million over five years. He saw Kenny Lofton turn down a $42 million offer, leading Hart to trade him after the 1996 season. He saw other players—among them Manny Ramirez and Jim Thome—approaching free agency. By the end of the 1998 season, Jacobs saw problems. The team was getting older. The payroll was going up. The stars were either going to break his self-imposed budget or leave as free agents. His reputation as a popular owner and his bottom line would both take a hit. Dick Jacobs was sixty-one when he bought the Indians after the 1986 season, and he was seventy-three after the 1998 season. Why endure the public relations agony of a team headed toward a decline?

As Jacobs once said, "I always felt the driving force behind a franchise is long-term growth. There's a time to hold, a time to fold."

And a time to deal.

And this would be one of the biggest, most profitable deals of his life.

CHAPTER 2

"YOU CAN'T WAIT FOR THE RIGHT TIME TO BUY THE INDIANS."

THE DOLAN FAMILY TAKES OVER

The Dolan family had franchise fever. That made them the perfect bidder for Dick Jacobs, the pure businessman. The fact that they were baseball fans from the Cleveland suburb of Chagrin Falls made them even more appealing. The Dolans had been trying to buy their way into professional sports for a few years. They were frustrated. They were hungry. They had money. They knew how the pro franchise game worked.

They finished right behind billionaire Al Lerner in the bidding for the expansion Cleveland Browns. They dealt with the National Football League, putting together a group that would have Hall of Fame coach Don Shula as president of football operations and Bill Cosby as a minor owner who would represent the minority interest that the league claimed was important. The real money came from Charles Dolan, brother of Larry Dolan. Charles, based in New York, was the owner of Cablevision, Madison Square Garden, and the New York Knicks. It was the power of Charles Dolan's checkbook that led the Dolans to offer $525 million for the Browns. The Browns went to Al Lerner for $530 million. This was in 1998, and it was the highest price ever paid for an American sports franchise.

Dick Jacobs was very aware of the Dolans' interest in sports. The Tribe owner himself had been among the early bidders for the Browns. Jacobs correctly saw the NFL as a place where only the likes of Art Modell could manage to lose money. It had everything Jacobs believed baseball needed in terms of financial structure: a salary cap, lucrative revenue sharing, long-term player contracts that usually were not guaranteed. But once the bidding went over $400 million, Jacobs was out.

The Dolans were discouraged when they lost out to Lerner, who seemed to be the favorite of the NFL establishment once the bidding became serious. Lerner had been Modell's old partner with the Browns. But after Modell moved to Baltimore (with the help of Lerner), there was a major split between the two men. In fact, Modell backed the Dolans in their bid for the expansion Browns.

"We made what was supposed to be a model bid," said Paul Dolan, current Indians president and son of Larry Dolan. "But every time we did something, they [the NFL] asked for something else. When Lerner became involved, we knew it was an uphill battle."

The Dolans learned a lot about the politics of pro sports by going through that process. Afterward, Charles Dolan seemed content to stay with his New York holdings, but Larry Dolan still wanted a piece of the pro sports action. His next move was to try to buy out Marge Schott's ownership of the Cincinnati Reds. With the help of former Indians assistant general manager Dan O'Dowd, Larry and Paul Dolan thought they had a deal for Schott's interest in the National League franchise. The Dolans would own the team. Paul Dolan would be team president, O'Dowd would run the baseball operation.

"We were going to own about 50 percent of the team," said Paul Dolan. "The minority owners had a thirty-day window to match our offer. They did."

They *hoped* they would own the Browns. They actually *believed* they'd own the Reds because there were no other serious bidders. In less than a year, they had nearly bought two teams—and ended up with none. We can't know for sure if Jacobs already had the Dolans in mind as possible buyers when he put the team up for sale in the spring of 1999. Jacobs doesn't talk about these issues. But consider Jacobs for a moment. He's shrewd. He knows all the money families in Cleveland. He had watched the Dolans finish second on two occasions bidding for teams, and he knew they bid $525 million for the Browns. He saw how hard they worked to purchase the Reds, a team to which they had no real emotional attachment. It's a safe bet that from the moment he announced the franchise was available, he believed the Dolans would be serious contenders.

The Dolans didn't want to take a third swing at a franchise and strike out.

"I was doing a case in court when Dan O'Dowd called to say the Indians were for sale," said Paul Dolan, a lawyer in his father's firm. "I knew it was our team. We had vetted the community when we bid for the Browns. We knew the competition. I felt we'd get it done."

The Dolans contacted Jacobs. They were told to talk to Goldman Sachs, the investment firm that would be handling the bidding for the franchise. End of conversation.

"My dad didn't know Dick Jacobs personally, nor did anyone in our family," said Paul Dolan. "This definitely was not a case where two businessmen who knew each other agreed to do a deal. It was negotiated. We came through the front door. They pushed us for a price."

This was vintage Jacobs. When bidding for the Browns, he saw how the NFL squeezed the bidders, drove up the price, and made sure that no one trying to buy the team knew exactly where they stood. It was an excellent tactic. He believed the fewer people who really knew his business, the better. Jacobs was in no hurry when he put the team up for sale in the spring of 1999. The Indians had already (again) sold out the season before the first pitch. He was looking at an $8 million profit, even assuming they didn't make the playoffs. He was reasonably sure they'd win the Central Division.

"Goldman Sachs provided the financial information on the team," said Paul Dolan. "The franchise was in great shape. We understood that it was close to being at its peak, and there would only be incremental growth. The new park was built. There were no more tickets to sell. No more revenue, short of raising ticket prices. It was very healthy and we'd be buying at its peak. If we were just thinking short term, we'd never do it. We were thinking long term."

As Dolan remembered this process, he paused. He tried to explain what his family was thinking.

"Baseball is a business unlike any other business," he said. "There are only thirty teams. Only one is the Cleveland Indians. It may come up for sale only once in a lifetime. You can't wait for the right time to buy the Indians. There may never be a right time. There is only the time when they are for sale."

The time was 1999, and these were *the Cleveland Indians*!

The Indians are special, if you have memories of watching Bob Feller at old League Park, as Larry Dolan did . . . or Rocky Colavito, Max Alvis, Larry Brown, and Sam McDowell at the old Cleveland Stadium, as Paul Dolan did. Being poised to buy the Indians is not a rational business moment for any Tribe fan who grew up in the Cleveland area. Remember that George Steinbrenner's first choice was not to buy the New York Yankees. He wanted the Indians, and thought his group had a deal with Vernon Stouffer in 1972. But emotionally Stouffer was a mess. His family business was falling apart, and the Tribe was losing. He nearly sold to Steinbrenner, but instead was hustled by Nick Mileti and a large cast of partners. Mileti never really had the cash to run the Tribe. Steinbrenner's next move was to New York, where he purchased the Yankees. This is the typical story for Tribe fans in the 1960s, 1970s, and 1980s. For all of Steinbrenner's bluster and obvious weaknesses, the man had access to money and the drive to field a contending team, a combination rare in Cleveland pro sports.

When Dick Jacobs bought the Indians in 1986, he knew he was making a shrewd investment. The Dolan family also bid for the Tribe in 1986. They offered about $28 million before dropping out. Twelve years later, their bid was now over $300 million and rising. Yes, Jacobs liked owning the Indians. But he loved making deals that made him money. Dick Jacobs never would have bought the Indians in 1999. Too little to gain, too much to lose. Which was exactly why he was selling. Now that he had lured the Dolans with the irresistible bait of a franchise the family had always dreamed of owning, he just played the waiting game.

"We never knew who else was bidding or what they were offering," said Paul Dolan.

One other bidder became public. It was the Ganley family, which owns several car dealerships in northern Ohio. A family member told me that when the bidding rose to $200 million, they realized they were in trouble. At $220 million, they backed out. It's possible there was another serious bidder, but none became public. There wasn't even a decent rumor. It appears that it was the Ganleys and the Dolans, then just the Dolans. But no one knew for sure, and that included the Dolans.

"There's an emotional premium, buying the team we grew up with," admitted Paul Dolan.

The final price was $320 million, at the time the most ever paid for a Major League Baseball franchise. The Dolans say they paid about $275 million in cash because there was some debt and there were other complicated financial parts of the sale. The Dolans also were able to keep all the advance ticket sales for the 2000 season, some of which came in during the final days of Jacobs's ownership before the sale to the Dolans became final. Even at $260 million cash (with the $15 million in ticket sales), the cost was high.

Larry Dolan was sixty-nine years old when the deal was finalized, but he wanted the franchise for his family. The plan had long been for Paul Dolan to be the hands-on presence in the front office, which he has been with the Indians.

Meanwhile, Jacobs had to clean up some final details of the sale. He carried about $35 million in personal debt against the team, which was allowed under Major League Baseball rules. He had never bothered to pay it back because he knew that he'd eventually sell for far more than the $35 million original purchase price. That piece of information makes it sound like Jacobs bought the team for no cash. But he did pay out the money, then borrowed it back later. He once told me that he lost about $40 million on the Indians before the Jacobs Field era. In the early years of Jacobs's ownership, he had to pay out $10 million as part of the Major League Baseball collusion settlement with the Players Association. Since the Indians were a private company, it's hard to know the real bottom line between 1987, when he bought the team, and 1993, the first year covered in the stock prospectus. A *Plain Dealer* story from May 3, 1992, reported the team lost $12 million in 1991. So it's very possible the $40 million loss figure is reasonably accurate. From 1995 to 1999, the team netted at least $60 million. That's an average of $12 million a year, not counting the money Jacobs pocketed from the initial public offering of stock. Dick Jacobs made a lot of great investments in his life, but this may have been the best.

The Dolans did know that the incredible growth could not continue. But they were just interested in owning the team, winning games, breaking even, and getting back to the World Series. They were going to run the Indians as much with their hearts as their heads. At the time of the purchase, no baseball team was ever sold for more money than the Indians. This was Cleveland, not New York or Chicago. It's not a boomtown, and it's only the sixteenth-largest TV market in the country. The Los Angeles Dodgers had been sold only a few months earlier for $311 million. So Dick Jacobs convinced the Dolans to buy the Indians for more than the megamarket Dodgers. Now you know why at the time the sale was announced, baseball commissioner Bud Selig told *USA Today*, "Dick Jacobs is one of the most constructive and smartest owners I've known in all my years of baseball."

A conservative estimate is that Jacobs cleared $300 million on the deal, when you factor in everything from what the Dolans paid to the profits made to the stock sale.

"Dick Jacobs is a single-minded, tough businessman," said Paul Dolan. "As a fan, I kind of thought he was a little too tight. But I've come to appreciate his ownership more over time. I've come to understand that his is the best way to run a franchise."

But at the time of the sale, the Dolans didn't know it.

"There isn't a fan who sits in those seats that wants a World Series more than I do," Larry Dolan said at a February 22, 2000, press conference. "I've talked to my family about the pressure of the only thing left to do being to win the World Series. We welcome the pressure because we want the same thing. We want to put a team together that can reasonably compete every fall for the World Series."

The fans and the media heard that and loved it. Dick Jacobs never talked like that. Dick Jacobs talked about contending, and putting together an entertaining team. But he also stressed that he was done losing money on the Indians once they moved into Jacobs Field. The Dolans would soon discover why Dick Jacobs never promised Tribe fans a World Series.

It began with Manny Ramirez.

CHAPTER 3

"MANNY'S FREE AGENCY WAS A CIRCUS."

THE DEPARTURE OF MANNY RAMIREZ

It was February 25, 2000. This was the Dolans' first press conference after officially taking over as owners of the Tribe. Larry Dolan loves to tell stories of watching the Indians at old League Park, of the 1948 and 1954 Tribe, of great family times at the old Cleveland Stadium. During this event, he even mentioned a game where the Indians beat Boston on a ninth-inning home run by the long-forgotten Ron Lolich.

Larry Dolan didn't remember the name, but son Paul Dolan supplied it.

Then Larry Dolan mentioned that he wanted to watch some of the games in the stands with the fans, just like Bill Veeck.

The man clearly had no idea what was coming.

Fans love to share their memories, and the Dolans are true-blue baseball fans. But once they bought the team, they learned a lot about fan mentality. It comes down to this: What have you done for me lately, and what will you do in the future?

No one cared that the Dolans gave the okay to Dick Jacobs to sign free agent pitcher Chuck Finley to a three-year, $27 million deal. Or that they agreed to sign Cuban import Danys Baez to a four-year, $14 million deal despite the fact that right-hander had never thrown a pitch in a pro game. Or that Robbie Alomar, Jim Thome, and Kenny Lofton all had contracts in the $7 million to $8 million range. Or that the 2000 payroll was $82 million, the highest in team history. The Dolans might have hoped for some sort of public acknowledgment that in their first year, they were spending more than Jacobs ever did. But they weren't going to get it.

In that first, fateful press conference, the questions were all about Manny Ramirez. Manny was the team's top talent and one of the best hitters in the game. He was also a fan favorite. And his contract would expire after the 2000 season. Could they sign him, or would he leave town as a free agent?

"If there's a way to keep Manny, we'll do it," Larry Dolan said.

I was covering that press conference, and when Dolan said those words, I thought, "Manny's gone."

As I wrote for the *Akron Beacon Journal* that day, "The answer to the Manny Question is simple—No . . . No, the Indians will not be able to keep Manny."

Word was already out: Manny had hired yet another agent—his fifth. Ramirez often changed agents when he made a new friend on the team and then met that player's agent. Usually, it was an older player whom Ramirez admired, and it wasn't hard for that agent to convince Ramirez that he needed new representation. Then it was up to the agents to work out a deal among themselves, and this sometimes had two agents convinced they were representing Ramirez—which was true, at least for a while. This time the new agent was Jeff Moorad, who had one goal in mind: He wanted to be the next Scott Boras. Many fans don't understand that the game within the game isn't just the strategy in the dugout or the front office. In modern baseball, the agents can be major players. Boras came to rule baseball by consistently signing players to the largest contracts—and then letting the world know it. Perhaps the only people whose egos are larger than the players are the super-agents such as Boras. And right behind Boras was Moorad. In the middle of this agent tug-of-war were Ramirez and the Indians.

It's doubtful the Dolans fully understood this on that day in late February. They also didn't comprehend what it's like in Manny's World. Manny Ramirez was not about to tell Jeff Moorad that he wanted to stay in Cleveland or anywhere else. Manny Ramirez never could connect the dots of life's big picture. His life was coming to the ballpark, taking batting practice, joking with his teammates, playing the game, driving in runs. He loved to hit, and paid attention to details about his stance, his swing, and what pitches he wanted to hit. But he cared little about what bat he used, often grabbing anything in the bat rack, swinging it a few times. If it felt good, he took it to home plate. It was not uncommon for Ramirez to use bats from two or three different players in the same game. Once, Ramirez was accused of corking his bat by an opposing team. The next day, I looked in his locker, and he had three bats—from three different teammates. He didn't even use his own model. The Manny Ramirez bats stood lonely in the rack, their owner ignoring them in favor of the wood that caught his attention on this day. So Manny corking bats? Whose bats? It was outrageous.

Tribe fans know some of the Manny stories. There was Manny stealing second, then walking back to first and being tagged out.

"I thought it was a foul ball," he said.

That was strange, since the batter, Jim Thome, didn't even swing.

Manny would wear his teammates' uniform pants. The baggier they looked, the better he liked them. He once asked *Beacon Journal* baseball writer Sheldon Ocker if he could borrow $60,000 so he and teammate Julian Tavarez could buy motorcycles. He asked a Tribe clubhouse guy to drive his car to get it washed, mentioning there was money in the glove compartment to pay for the wash. The clubhouse guy opened the glove box and sure enough there was money. Lots of money. About $10,000 in $100 bills.

Before the 2000 season, Ken Griffey instructed his agent to give the Reds a hometown discount so he could work out a deal to keep Griffey in Cincinnati. That led to a nine-year, $116 million deal. Moorad immediately dismissed that type of contract. He talked about waiting until the end of the season, and getting "market value" for Ramirez. Whenever you hear an agent say that about a Cleveland player, you know that he's gone. "Market value" means taking the player to a bigger market in a larger city where they can pay more money. What the Indians also didn't know was that Moorad decided to allow ESPN to film some of his telephone conversations during the Ramirez negotiations with different teams. No one can be positive of Moorad's intent, but it certainly did serve as a commercial for himself, especially if he could produce a monster contract for his new client.

When Larry Dolan was speaking at that February press conference, the biggest blast of free agent contracts in baseball history was only months away. A hint came when the Dodgers signed Shawn Green—a productive player but no Ramirez—to a six-year deal worth nearly $80 million. If Green netted about $13 million a year, Ramirez was going to come close to being a $20 million a year player. The Indians had to know that. They did sense they were in trouble.

In retrospect, the smartest move might have been to trade Ramirez during that spring training. But this was 2000. The Indians had just won 97 games in 1999, but collapsed in the first round of the playoffs. They were expected to contend again. The Dolans were taking over a team that had sold out 373 consecutive games and were on the verge of selling out yet another season before opening day. It was a team that had won the Central Division from 1995 to 1999. If ownership decided to dump Ramirez for some prospects, it would have been viewed as running up a surrender flag, a betrayal of the fans who were paying out big bucks for tickets before the first pitch of the season. There would have been a fan and media rebellion if the new owners had traded Ramirez right after assuming full control of the team, even if it was better business in the long run. When the Dolans' ownership began, their thinking was win now, let tomorrow worry about itself. They had to ride it out with Ramirez, much like the Indians had done with Albert Belle in 1996. That season, Jacobs and Hart knew that Belle, their best hitter, would be gone at the end of the year via free agency. But they had just been to the 1995 World Series and wanted to return. Belle would not bring anything near full value in a trade because he was in the final year of his contract and could leave at the end of the season. So the Indians kept Belle, hoping he'd have a huge year (he did), and hoping he could carry them back to the World Series (he didn't).

The 2000 season was frustrating for the Tribe. They started slowly, reaching a 44–42 record at the All-Star break. After the All-Star break, they went 46–30, the best in the American League. Their final record was a strong 90–72, but that put them five games behind the Chicago White Sox in the Central Division. They missed the wild card playoff berth by a single game. John Hart made several midseason trades trying to squeeze out one more playoff appearance. He brought in veterans Wil Cordero, David Segui, Jason Bere, Steve Woodard, and Bob Wickman. Future slugger Richie Sexson left the Indians as part of the deal with Milwaukee for Wickman, Bere, and Woodard. Cordero had been with the Indians in 1999, and Tribe management laughed when Pittsburgh gave him a three-year, $9 million deal in the winter. They thought the Pirates had wildly overpaid. Then seven months later, desperate for another bat, they traded infielder Enrique Wilson and minor league prospect Alex Ramirez for Cordero. Now they were stuck with Cordero's contract. These moves show no thought given to the future. Win now, pay for it later. Which they did as Sexson developed into a star for Milwaukee while only Wickman in return became a long-term member of the Indians. Cordero chewed up $3 million annually as a backup outfielder.

The Dolans were going along with Hart's moves because they were desperate to return to the playoffs. They didn't want the team to miss the playoffs—and the postseason money—in the first year of their watch.

But it happened. The 2000 playoffs came, the Indians stayed home.

"We came in more as fans, and that's why we signed Finley and Baez and made some of the other moves," said Paul Dolan. "We sort of threw out the window the Jacobs approach of building in a profit. Then we saw the team virtually collapse in the first couple of months—that gave us a feeling of a deer in the headlights. We knew the club didn't have much left in it, but we thought we had enough hitting and if we could add some pitching, we could get over the hump."

Dolan said the Indians under Dick Jacobs never budgeted for any playoff money, but it was "wink-wink," because they were reasonably certain they'd pick up anywhere from $2 million to $5 million, depending upon how deep they went into the playoffs. A seven-game World Series could boil up the postseason pot to as much as $8 million.

The 2000 Tribe never even got to nibble on a playoff appetizer. They went through a major league record 32 pitchers. They had three go on the disabled list in one day. As I wrote at one point that season, the Indians had had nearly as many MRIs as RBI. Despite the strong finish, the team was getting old, physically breaking down.

"We lost about $10 million that year, and we did it with an $82 million payroll," said Paul Dolan. "We didn't like losing that much money. We felt a little uneasy. There was a point in the season where we lost to Detroit, and David Justice said the window [of opportunity] was closing on the team. We immediately denied that was the case, but there was a lot [of truth] to that. After we missed the playoffs, we were very aware the window was closing, but we felt we still had an opportunity to do something with the current club. That's when we decided to really go hard after Manny."

The Dolans did not want the Indians to fall apart on their watch. Manny Ramirez had a stunning 2000 season, hitting .351 with 38 homers and 122 RBI in 118 games. He missed 44 games because of a hamstring injury, something that really bothered Hart, who criticized Ramirez in the media for not coming back sooner. That seemed unfair, as Ramirez had averaged 150 games per season from 1996 to 1999. Manny liked to play, and this was his first trip to the disabled list in his big league career. There were whispers that he may have been cautious about returning too fast because he didn't want to re-injure his leg and ruin his statistics for free agency. It's doubtful that Ramirez thought that deeply. Besides, even on one leg, Manny hit. In his final at-bat in the 2000 season, he homered 450 feet to deep center field. He received a standing ovation when he came to the plate, and an even louder cheer as he rounded the bases. The fans sensed he would be gone. The Dolans found themselves caught up in the emotion. They may have not made the playoffs, but they were going to keep Ramirez.

"During the season, we had concluded that we were not going to re-sign Manny and were really focused elsewhere," said Paul Dolan. "We initially made some proposals because we felt we needed to make some proposals, but we had no expectations they would be accepted. But somewhere along the line, we became engaged in wanting to get him. In doing so, we acted irrationally."

This was the winter that Scott Boras negotiated the $252 million contract for Alex Rodriguez with the Texas Rangers. It was when Derek Jeter signed a deal worth $17 million annually to stay with the Yankees. Toronto signed Carlos Delgado to a four-year, $68 million deal, averaging $17 million annually. Jeff Moorad was determined to make Ramirez the second-highest-paid player in the game, behind Rodriguez but ahead of everyone else. Moorad was a regular guest on Cleveland-area talk shows. He made himself available to the media covering the Tribe. He was hyping Ramirez, insisting his client had a genuine interest in staying with the Tribe—if only they'd offer a little more. Okay, a *lot* more!

It became a duel between the Indians and Boston.

"We started at something like $70 million for seven years," said Paul Dolan. "Then we were up to something like $115 million for eight years. Boston kept raising their offer. We got caught up in it. We were telling ourselves, 'Hey, we can get this guy!' My father clearly was driving it, as John Hart was prepared to move on [without Ramirez]. But when John saw my father driving it, he caught the fever, too."

Boston began at $122 million for seven years, then raised it to a staggering eight-year, $160 million deal. That made Ramirez a $20 million a year player, second only to Rodriguez, exactly what Moorad wanted.

The Indians countered with their own eight-year, $160 million contract. Only $120 million was to be paid in the first eight years, the rest in deferred payments in the future.

"Even with the $40 million deferred, there really was no way we could afford to pay Manny and put any team around him," said Paul Dolan. "At least, not if we were looking at it realistically. But we rationalized it by forecasting forward, assuming we'd continue to draw at least 3 million fans a year for the next eight years. We got caught up in the competition and lost our objectivity. You get caught up in the game agents play as they get the market stirred up and that got us stirred up."

Chris Antonetti had just joined the Indians in 1999 as an assistant in baseball operations, not a very high position. His specialty is numbers, and he's good at it. He is also a shrewd analyst, which is why he quickly rose to the position of assistant general manager in the Mark Shapiro regime. After the 2005 season, he interviewed for the open general manager's job in Philadelphia, a real compliment to someone only thirty years old.

In those first years with the Tribe, Antonetti sensed storm clouds forming over the franchise.

"We were in something like the sixteenth-largest media market, but our payroll was fourth in baseball," he said. "There was a string of unprecedented sellouts, but at some point, all good things come to an end . . . It is unreasonable to expect you're going to continue to sell out eighty-one baseball games a year in perpetuity. It's just not going to happen."

That was a clear assessment, and it wouldn't be long until that prediction ultimately proved true. The Dolans knew this, but they wanted to avoid it.

"Had Manny taken our offer, it would have been devastating to the franchise," said Paul Dolan. "We were very lucky. This could have been a case study about why teams get in trouble when dealing with free agents."

Had it truly been up to Ramirez, he may indeed have accepted the offer. He never wanted to leave Cleveland. This was his comfort zone. But as Tribe broadcaster Tom Hamilton said, "Manny's free agency was a circus. Jeff Moorad was in a battle against Scott Boras. It was ego against ego for who would be number one. I really thought Manny would stay because of his comfort level here, but Manny didn't make the decision. You knew he wouldn't make that decision."

Moorad used the Indians to drive up the price for Boston, then he cut the deal with the Red Sox.

"It was just Boston and us," Hart told me right at the end of the negotiations. "We had to backload the contract. We couldn't offer a $16 million signing bonus like Boston did. Boston was desperate. Their team was for sale. They have a lucrative cable TV deal. They had to do something."

The first five years of the Boston deal paid Ramirez $108 million en route to that $160 million over eight years.

The Indians found themselves in the middle of a changing baseball economy. No longer was the bottom line primarily built on how many fans were in the seats. Cable television networks were supplying major dollars. Boston and New York were making ten times as much money from their cable deals as the Tribe. The reason Texas put $252 million in the hands of Rodriguez was that the Rangers were putting together a cable network and they wanted Rodriguez to be a star enticing more stations to sign up.

"Look at what happened two years later," said Paul Dolan. "Manny's contract became such a burden, Boston put him on waivers just hoping someone would claim him. Now, my father and the rest of us realize this could have been a huge mistake, and we won't get caught up in something like that again."

Ramirez continued to be an elite slugger, yet no one wanted to take on the final six years and $120 million of his deal. In Texas, after three years the Rangers found they couldn't pay Rodriguez and have enough left to put a contending team around him. They ended up trading their star to the only team that could afford him—the Yankees.

"And Texas paid some of A-Rod's salary to get that deal done," said Antonetti. "Had we signed Manny, we could have ended up trying to trade him—and probably paying part of the contract just to make it happen."

While the Ramirez negotiations were taking place, the Dolans actually were spending more money. They signed thirty-six-year-old Ellis Burks to a three-year, $19.5 million deal. He had hit .344 with 24 homers and 96 RBI for San Francisco, but it was no secret that Burks had horrible knees and would be limited to being a designated hitter. So he'd be forty when the contract was finished, a major gamble on a guy whose health was already questionable. But the Indians wanted back into the playoffs, and hoped Burks would partly replace some of the offense they lost to Ramirez.

Then another agent stepped in with a new idea.

Scott Boras represented Juan Gonzalez, a former two-time Most Valuable Player who was coming off the worst season of his ten-year career. Gonzalez batted .289 with 22 homers and 67 RBI for Detroit, where he had turned down an eight-year, $140 million offer early in the 2000 season. Then he was bothered by injuries and distracted by a losing team and the huge Detroit ballpark with deep fences that he was certain cost him home runs. He was an unhappy guy and played with an alarmingly passive attitude for an athlete in a free-agent year. Most teams thought, "If he can't play hard and produce when his contract is up, why would he do it any other time?"

Boras watched the Ramirez negotiations. He knew the Indians were prepared to offer Ramirez more than $10 million in the first year of that contract. He suggested taking that $10 million and giving it to Gonzalez.

One year, $10 million. If he plays well, we can talk about an extension. If not, you only have him for one year. That was the Boras sales pitch.

The Indians were buyers once again.

"Signing Gonzalez was one of our better moves because he had a great year [.325, 35 homers, 140 RBI]," said Paul Dolan. "But it brought our payroll up to $96 million."

Think about this for a moment. The Indians lost Ramirez, their best hitter. Yet, their payroll *rose* from $82 million to $96 million. Making it even worse, the Dolans were being called cheapskates by the fans because they couldn't keep Ramirez. They went into the 2001 season with an old team, as Omar Vizquel, Travis Fryman, Chuck Finley, Charles Nagy, Dave Burba, Steve Reed,

Robbie Alomar, Kenny Lofton, Burks, and Gonzalez were all at least thirty-one. In fact, the starting lineup in the field was the second oldest in the American League. The Indians were taking one last shot at the World Series. They were throwing all their chips on the table. In spring training Vizquel was predicting they'd win 100 games. Manager Charlie Manuel was insisting they'd win the Central Division.

They won 91 games. They won the Central Division. They lost to Seattle in the first round of the playoffs.

When the Tribe clinched the 2001 Central Division title, I started my newspaper column:

> Tribe fans, enjoy this.
>
> Never take a championship, any championship, as your rightful inheritance. Don't fall into the trap of thinking every Indian summer will be like this one, because it won't.
>
> This will be the sixth Central Division title in seven years. It's a team that has won 13 games at Jacobs Field in its last at-bat. It's a team with an MVP candidate (Gonzalez) in right field, an MVP candidate (Alomar) at second base and a possible 50-homer muscleman (Jim Thome) at first . . . with maybe the greatest defensive shortstop (Omar Vizquel) ever to wear a glove.
>
> This is not a perfect team, but a fun team. A team that, in the words of GM John Hart, "gives us something to talk about around the coffee maker at the office."
>
> It's a team where no lead is safe, the opposition's or its own. It's a team that has blown countless 5-run advantages, yet has come back from 12 runs behind to win, and it was against Seattle, the best team in baseball! It's Hart's last team and it reflects the personality of the man who deserves the monster share of the credit for a great baseball revival that began with the move to Jacobs Field in 1994.

Some of us read that and shrug.

Some say, "Well, they never won a World Series, so if they ask me, they ain't won nothin' yet."

Some people don't have a clue . . .

I didn't have a clue, either. I didn't understand they were spending at an unprecedented rate, almost like a person who keeps signing up for one credit card, charging to the maximum, then signing up for another card . . . and another. For a while, the expensive toys are fun, but then the bills come due—with interest.

CHAPTER 4

"WE DIDN'T HAVE ENOUGH FINGERS FOR ALL THE LEAKS."

THE ROBERTO ALOMAR TRADE

After the 2001 season, the Indians had a great player to trade in All-Star second baseman Robbie Alomar.

Problem was, they couldn't decide what kind of trade they wanted to make. So they made two different types of trades in one, and that rarely works. The team was getting old and going downhill, as there weren't enough young players coming up. Every member of the Tribe front office knew it as they watched their team limp out of the first round of the 2001 playoffs. This was a five-game series the Indians could have won, maybe even should have won. They were up 2-1 in the series, having just crushed Seattle 17–2 at Jacobs Field. They had Bartolo Colon set to pitch Game 4 at home, which should have been the clincher. Colon took a 1–0 lead into the seventh inning, then gave up three runs. The bullpen coughed up three more in what became a 6–2 loss.

Suddenly, the series was tied.

The Indians flew to Seattle for the fifth and deciding game, and they were utterly helpless against Jamie Moyer, the ageless Mariner whose pitches were more like soft rolling waves than roaring fastballs. The Indians never seemed to hit the guy, and nothing was different on this day.

The game saw Robbie Alomar ground into a double play, then jog to first base. He probably would not have been safe had he hustled, but the image was haunting. It seemed like Alomar had given up. It seemed like the team had given up. Or maybe just run out of gas. I was in Seattle that day, and it was obvious that more than a season had ended. This was also the final chapter of the Indians as the fans came to know them during the 1990s.

Here's part of what I wrote after that game:

> So this is how the season ends.
>
> John Hart standing in the middle of the Tribe clubhouse that's so quiet, you could almost hear a heart break as he talked about his final day as the team's general manager.
>
> Kenny Lofton in front of his locker, taking off his Wahoo uniform probably for the last time in his career.
>
> Charlie Manuel sitting in his office, skin a pasty white, eyes a little blood-shot red. He rubs his weary face. His future as manager probably will be determined by a physical at the end of the season. He has been in the hospital five times in the last two years, mostly with colon problems.
>
> Juan Gonzalez is nowhere to be found. Like Lofton, he is a free agent who probably will be gone next year.
>
> Travis Fryman knows his next stop is shoulder surgery. Dave Burba has no idea where he will be pitching next year, but it probably won't be in Cleveland. John Rocker is in baseball limbo, probably headed elsewhere assuming the Indians can find someone to take him.
>
> Hart will soon interview for the GM job in Texas. Gonzalez has hired Jeff Moorad, the same agent who led Manny Ramirez to Boston. Ownership has made noise about cutting payroll, or at least not raising it . . .

The story went on to say the Indians still should be favored to win the Central Division in 2002, but "the old bash-and-mash Tribe is changing."

As I read that story years after I wrote it, I know I sensed the same impending doom as the front office. And just like the front office, I didn't want to admit it. Winning was too much fun, and if they really couldn't win as big as they once did, I was willing to settle for the illusion of winning.

In the owners' office, Larry and Paul Dolan were doing more than assessing a 91–71 season and a Central Division title. They were staring at the real bottom line.

"We had lost nearly $20 million," said Paul Dolan.

The unprecedented, baseball record–setting 455-game sell-out streak had come to an end. The Indians still drew 3,175,523 fans, still sold out 35 games. But they could see some slippage of support coming. Not every luxury box was being sold. Not every season ticket was being renewed. Not every game at Jacobs Field was considered an event.

Reality was returning.

"We realized that our market could only sustain a payroll in the $70 million range unless we were going to the World Series every year," said Paul Dolan.

Former owner Dick Jacobs would have agreed. His final payroll was $72 million in 1999.

"We came in and tried to sustain the winning by spending like the Yankees," said Paul Dolan. "The Yankees have a way of just spending through their issues, just buying more players, and eventually their payroll was more than $200 million. We knew we couldn't do business like that."

Change was coming.

"From the day we bought the team, John Hart was telling us that we were going to have to turn the team over, get younger," said Paul Dolan. "The question was how long could we push that day of reckoning away? After the 2001 season, we knew it was coming."

They sort of knew. Certainly Hart did, which was why he was glad to leave the Indians on a good note and take big bucks to run the Texas Rangers. He knew what needed to be done, and he knew the fans and media would scream. He knew it would be hard, and he really just didn't want to deal with it at this point of his career. He was fifty-three and, like every other baseball fan in Cleveland, hooked on winning. So he headed to Texas.

That left the thirty-four-year-old Mark Shapiro to figure out what to do next.

"I told the Dolans that at some point, we were headed toward a rebuilding process," said Shapiro. "I didn't know if it was in 2002 or 2003, but a painful process was coming. We did not have enough talent in the upper levels of our farm system. It was coming, the question was 'When?'"

The answer no one wanted to hear was, "Right now!" That was especially true when the Dolans said payroll had to be cut. They had lost about $30 million in two years since buying the team. But they were afraid if they went into a complete rebuilding mode, it would destroy ticket sales for 2002. And that would lead to even heavier financial losses.

"Now I realize we didn't confront it totally," said Paul Dolan. "We labeled it as 'Transition.' The idea was we could contend and rebuild at the same time."

Fat chance.

That's like saying you want to lose weight and you will give up those cookies on the weekend, but you're still eating some ice cream every day.

"I honestly felt we had a chance to contend in 2002," said Shapiro three years later.

Okay, but contend for what? Maybe a playoff spot? And all the while, knowing that the real work of rebuilding still had not been done. The problem was the foundation of the house was rotting, but the Indians wanted to just fix the holes in the roof and hope to make it through another winter.

But then what? The foundation still had to be dug up and replaced. Even if the Indians did slip into the playoffs, they didn't have the kind of talent to win a World Series. And the following year, the situation would just be worse.

"People were already calling us cheap because we had lost Ramirez [in 2001] and we weren't going to bring back Juan Gonzalez," said Paul Dolan. "We were coming off a $96 million payroll. That was one of the top five in baseball, the highest in team history. We could be called a lot of things, but not cheap."

What they needed to be was gutsy and visionary. They had to do business a new way. Shapiro knew it, he just wasn't sure exactly how and when to do it. That was on his mind as he headed to the Winter Meetings wanting to make a deal that would help both the present and the future.

He knew that Robbie Alomar already seemed to be going into a funk about the direction of the franchise. Alomar had two years left on a contract at $8 million annually, rather reasonable for an All-Star, Gold Glove second baseman. Alomar was coming off a brilliant year in 2001, hitting .336 with 20 homers, 100 RBI, and 30 stolen bases. The Indians were hearing that he wanted a new contract. Shapiro knew that the payroll was headed down, not up. He also knew the team was headed down, not up. And he knew Alomar would not like it, despite a postseason meeting in which Alomar said he would be okay with rebuilding. Maybe he was being sincere, but history showed that he tended to grow discontented, which is why the Indians were his fourth team. Rarely does a player so gifted move so much, unless there are other circumstances—namely, his attitude.

"We never thought Robbie was done as a player," said Shapiro. "I thought he'd play very well wherever he went. But he had two years left on his contract, and we thought that would maximize his value and bring more in return—rather than waiting until the final year of his contract. It wasn't that I worried about him not being on board with what we were doing. We needed to get some prospects, and I also wanted to get a proven big league player."

Shapiro was still assembling his management team. He inherited manager Charlie Manuel and virtually all of the scouts from the John Hart era. He was still getting to know ownership, especially Paul Dolan, who was taking the most active role in the team. It was Paul Dolan who was in the office virtually every day, while his father showed up about once a week. It was Paul Dolan to whom Shapiro spoke the most. Shapiro knew that Paul Dolan was on board with trading Alomar. But he also knew that ownership wasn't ready to write off the season, and neither was the first-year general manager.

"The truth was our pro scouting staff wasn't evolved to the point it is now," said assistant general manager Chris Antonetti. "We had just started reinvesting in our minor league scouting. We didn't have the depth of scouting that you'd like. We went through our reports and made a list of ten to twelve players that we liked."

Antonetti said Texas was the first target, and not just because John Hart was running the Rangers. Frank Catalanotto was one of the players mentioned, but the Rangers didn't seem desperate to deal for Alomar, or willing to part with the type of prospect that intrigued the Tribe. The Indians were shopping for a team that was obsessed with Alomar, and soon that team emerged. Mets general manager Steve Phillips just loved Alomar. He had started talking to Shapiro about the second baseman during the World Series, and kept at it when baseball's Winter Meeting began in early December. Phillips had lots of bodies, and he had a player the Indians had always liked—Matt Lawton.

Now here is where the Indians' scouting fell short. The Indians loved Lawton partly because he always hit so well against them. His career average against the Tribe was .324 with 9 homers and 46 RBI. Those were his best numbers against any American League team. Some said Lawton was a product of the artificial turf in Minnesota's Metrodome, where ground balls scooted far faster through the infield than they did on regular grass. The

Metrodome also was hitter friendly, especially in right field. But Lawton had a career average of .276 at Jacobs Field, compared to .285 at the Metrodome. So that didn't seem to be a deal breaker.

The consensus of several Tribe scouting reports on Lawton came down to this:

> Solid everyday Major League player . . . Lefthanded hitter has a little bit of a pull approach . . . FB hitter, but has shown the ability to make adjustments at the plate . . . Does not handle lefthanded pitching well, but should stay in the lineup. Does not profile as a power corner guy . . . uses speed at plate and the turf helped him . . . Solid average outfielder with speed and reactions to be a plus defender in the corner outfield . . . Definite interest on a speed-energy based club.

But the Indians should have dug deeper. They should have asked why Minnesota traded Lawton in the middle of the 2001 season when he was hitting .293 with 51 RBI in 103 games. Minnesota picked up pitcher Rick Reed, who was solid but not spectacular. He had an 8–6 record and 3.48 ERA at the time of the deal, but he was thirty-six and nearing the end of his career. They should have really wondered why Lawton then batted only .246 with three homers and 13 RBI in 183 at-bats for the Mets. The common reasoning was Lawton had never played in the National League before, so he didn't know the pitchers. This also was the first time he had been traded, and that sometimes sends players into shock for a few months. He was only thirty, so he should have been in his prime.

Confession time: I saw a lot of Lawton, and I saw much of what the Indians did. He hit the ball hard a lot. He drew a lot of walks and was consistently in the top 25 percent in on-base percentage. He seemed to hustle, play an above-average right field, and have a knack of hitting in the clutch. For his career, he was a .293

hitter with runners in scoring position, and .380 with the bases loaded. A lefty hitter, he seemed to handle all types of pitching during his career—.271 vs. lefties, .276 vs. righties.

But had the Indians been more diligent, they would have discovered the Twins were worried that Lawton's chunky body (five feet ten, 200 pounds) could be prone to injuries. He also was headed to arbitration, and only a year away from free agency. Minnesota did not believe he was worth a long-term investment, and the Twins usually are very savvy when it comes to judging their own players. His outfield play should have been put under the dreaded category of diminishing skills. He was losing speed and arm strength.

The Indians, however, were sold on Lawton.

"John Hart told me that he often had a gut feeling about certain players," said Shapiro. "John's strength was as a talent evaluator. He had played and managed in the minors. He could just tell about some players because of his background. I didn't have the same background, but I did have a gut feeling on Lawton. I liked his on-base percentage. I liked that he was not a 'swing-and-miss' guy, he made contact. This guy played great against us. I thought he was a team player."

They also were enamored with Alex Escobar, one of the minor league center fielders they scouted during the summer of 2002 when they eventually traded for Milton Bradley. Escobar was considered a superb prospect, though there were some warning signals.

Here was the Tribe's consensus report on Escobar:

> Athletic, multi-tooled player . . . can impact the game offensively and defensively . . . instinctive, lots of natural ability . . . chance to hit for average and power, but need[s] some adjustments at plate. Below average strike zone recognition and discipline . . . swings through fastballs up and breaking balls away . . . quick extension and enough bat

speed to handle the whole strike zone . . . defensive package and tools are an asset . . . Can handle CF on an everyday basis with a chance to be a Gold Glove in RF . . . Impressive combo of bat/power/ run/gold glove defense. Big upside, but not quite ready to have an impact role. Needs more seasoning.

Remember all the reasons the Indians said they liked Lawton? None of that applied to Escobar. He struck out, and struck out a lot. How about 146 strikeouts in 397 at-bats at Class AAA Norfolk? That's a horrible ratio, as he whiffed every 2.7 at-bats. Reaching base? He had only 35 walks in 111 games. He was supposed to have tremendous power, but he hit only 12 homers and drove in 52 runs with a .267 average in those 111 games. Granted, when he homered, the ball was picked up on the radar screen at NASA. In 2000, he played at Class AA Binghamton and struck out 114 times in 437 at-bats, compared to 57 walks. He did hit 16 homers, but these are scary numbers. The power was inconsistent, the walks too few, the strikeouts too constant. The Indians correctly pointed out that he was in Class AAA at the age of twenty-two, when many players were just coming out of college. The highly respected *Baseball America* magazine rated Escobar as the number one prospect in the Mets system, number eighteen in all of baseball. So the Indians weren't the only ones in love with the guy. He could run and played all three outfield positions. But the scouting report above says he *could* impact the game—it says very little about what he actually did. It was all projection, little production.

I didn't like Escobar from the moment the deal was announced as I studied his statistics. They were nearly as appalling as those of perpetual Tribe prospect Russell Branyan, who at least hit far more homers than Escobar—despite striking out nearly as often at Class AAA. If a guy strikes out every 2.7 times in the International League, how is he going to hit in the major leagues? Why would it be any better? It is far likely to be much worse. The six-foot-one, 180-pound Escobar physically looked like a star, and his fluid stride was an indication of innate athleticism. But something was missing.

"Escobar was the key guy in the trade," Shapiro admitted three years later.

The Mets also added Billy Traber, a Jamie Moyer–type soft-tossing lefty who had a 10–9 record and a 3.09 ERA in his first year of pro ball, pitching at all three minor league levels. He was the Mets' first-round draft pick in 2000, but a physical before he signed indicated a problem with his left elbow. His signing bonus was cut from $1.7 million to $400,000 because doctors believed that he'd need surgery at some point, but no one was sure when that would happen. I liked Traber because he averaged seven strikeouts and only two walks per nine innings, regardless of how unimpressive his readings were on the radar gun.

The Indians reports on Traber were mixed:

> Fastball was short, topping out at 88 mph. Mostly straight and up in the zone. Curveball lacked bite and velocity. Changeup was best pitch, he faded it with good deception. Control OK . . . Arm does not always catch up with his body leaving pitches up in the zone . . . Former first round pick who hurt his arm.

New York kept piling on players. There was Jerrod Riggan, a twenty seven-year-old reliever who had a 3.40 ERA in 47 innings with the Mets in 2001. There was Earl Snyder, a 25-year-old first baseman who had hit 73 homers in three previous minor league seasons. But he was rated just a marginal major league prospect.

The Indians scouts said Riggan had "average arm strength with above average straight fastball. Has a heavy 2-seam fastball with tail and sink . . . Problem is command and needs to be more consistent, has enough to be a long man out of the pen."

Snyder's defense was questionable, scouts admitting he had no real position. They thought he could be "a bench player" because of his bat. This was not a ringing endorsement.

The column I wrote on the day of the trade began: "I heard it, and I cringed. Robbie Alomar to the Mets for a bunch of guys."

I tried to give Shapiro and the Indians the benefit of the doubt, and I did like Lawton. But I sensed they didn't maximize Alomar's trade value. Tribe broadcaster Tom Hamilton had the same initial response, "I don't know if I should say it, but I just wasn't that excited about it. I said that to one of our front-office people, and they told me that it would work out. Then we started 11–1 in 2002, so what did I know? But it didn't take long to see that the team needed a complete overhaul. We were just trying to put fingers in a leaky dike, and we didn't have enough fingers for all the leaks."

They then made it worse by immediately signing Lawton to a four-year, $27 million contract extension. That meant they weren't even going to save any real money with the deal. Alomar was due to make $8 million over the next two years, and the Indians were committed to Lawton for four more years at nearly $7 million annually. They also signed journeyman second baseman Ricky Gutierrez to a three-year, $12 million deal. Add Lawton and Gutierrez together, and the Indians invested $11 million in 2002 for two rather average players.

This was not how to rebuild a franchise.

Trading Alomar, yes. Especially if you use him to restock your farm system. But adding Lawton and Gutierrez and paying them $11 million over the next three seasons?

"In defense of Mark, this was the year after Manny Ramirez [$160 million from Boston] and Alex Rodriguez [$252 million from Texas] signed those huge contracts, so the market was just crazy," said Paul Dolan. "Lawton seemed like the kind of guy who'd anchor our outfield for a long time. Gutierrez was a steady player. I liked the trade."

Shapiro now knows why it was a mistake.

"This was the more traditional way of doing business at that time," he said. "It's the way the Yankees still do business. You do the deal, and you immediately want to get the guy under contract to justify the trade you just made. You don't want to lose him to free agency in a year or two. We extended Lawton in twenty minutes on a plane. We had a good relationship with his agent, and we called and did it. This was done just before the industry went through a major overhaul and average players like Lawton began to fall back [in receiving long contracts] . . . Now, it's seems unbelievable that we did this. At that point, we were just doing what everyone else did, but we couldn't afford to do it how everyone else does it."

Tribe fans know what happened.

The 2002 Indians bolted from the gate with an 11–1 start, then things fell apart. Lawton separated his right shoulder while diving for a ball in the outfield on April 19. He took cortisone shots and played through much of the pain. He also pulled a calf muscle and went on the disabled list in July. In September, he had shoulder surgery. He batted .236 with 15 homers and 57 RBI. He had only one good year for the Tribe, and that was in 2004. His outfield play was abysmal. After the shoulder surgery, he couldn't throw. He used to have above-average speed, but no more. He battled injuries.

This was the first time he'd ever had a long-term contract, and he arrived in spring training about fifteen pounds overweight. Did the contract have anything to do with his lack of conditioning and injuries? Who knows, but Lawton certainly didn't play with the same fire that he did in Minnesota.

It was even worse for Gutierrez, who by August was out with a neck problem that required surgery. While he came back and played, he was never a regular.

Escobar struck out a lot, and had one injury after another.

Riggan and Snyder didn't contribute at the major league level.

Heading into 2006, not one player from the deal remained with the Tribe. The last to go was Traber, who indeed needed elbow surgery. He had it in 2004 and began his comeback in the minors in 2005. No one is sure if he will become a useful big league pitcher. He was hit hard at Class AAA Buffalo, then signed with the Washington Nationals as a minor league free agent before spring training in 2006.

Alomar quickly lost his edge. He was barely an average player after the Indians traded him, and then he retired in the spring of 2005.

This was a lousy trade for both teams.

It was a deal designed to please everyone—ownership and fans who wanted to contend now, and the baseball people who knew the farm system was barren and needed help. Like most such endeavors, it pleased almost no one.

"We just didn't have the information we needed," Shapiro said. "I look now at how we researched Gutierrez. I went on some very, very, very good information from a source that I trusted. The source commented about his makeup and character. He seemed to fit into the type of player that we needed. His numbers were pretty good, but we had very limited scouting looks at him. We didn't do our medical diligence well enough."

To the Indians' credit, they did spend a lot of time analyzing this trade *after* it was made. They did it with objectivity and with a mission to figure out where they went wrong, rather than falling into the hopeless hole of rationalizations and excuses.

"Chris [Antonetti] didn't caution me about signing Gutierrez for one year, or even the dollars, but he did caution me about the extra years," said Shapiro. "At the time, these guys were getting those kind of deals. But now I can see our process was flawed."

They didn't have extensive scouting reports on Gutierrez, which seemed strange. When they signed him as a free agent, he had been in the majors for eight seasons, all in the National League. He had been with three different teams. His lifetime average was .267, with little power. He had been on the disabled list four times between 1997 and 2000, although he was healthy in 2001, when he had one of his best seasons, batting .290 and leading the league with 17 sacrifice bunts playing for the Cubs. But Gutierrez was thirty-one, and there was nothing to indicate he was special, or on the verge of becoming so. Some teams offered him a two-year contract; the Indians went for three years.

They should have said, "There are a lot of guys out there like Ricky Gutierrez, why are we bidding for him? Let someone else sign him."

Antonetti said they learned much from the Lawton contract.

"You don't immediately acquire a player and give him an extension," he said. "We now take time to evaluate a player, to judge his work habits and attitude, things you really don't know until you have him and are around him every day. Also, don't make moves by emotion. You trade for a guy, so obviously you like him. You are excited by your trade. This is not a time to talk about an extension, because if the trade was a mistake, you can really compound it with a new contract . . . In retrospect, the biggest problem with the Robbie deal was the contracts [to Lawton and Gutierrez] given out."

No, the real problem was a lack of focus. Someone needed the courage to say what the Indians would six months later when they traded Bartolo Colon, namely, "We are in full rebuilding mode. We need the best prospects, period. We just have to take the hit. We're not going to win big with this team, so why not make the moves to try and build a viable contender in the future?"

The Indians also realized that there were "red flags," in Antonetti's words, about Escobar's physical conditions, because he did have back problems in the minors. It also should have given the Indians pause that the Mets were so willing to write off their supposed top prospect at the age of twenty-two. As Shapiro mentioned, several teams had a sincere interest in Escobar. He received a couple of calls from general managers wanting to trade for him right after Escobar had been acquired. But why didn't the excessive strikeouts and lack of walks and run production at Class AAA send off louder alarm bells? They would now, as the Indians pay more attention to on-base percentage in their player evaluations.

They knew Traber was a gamble, but thought he was worth taking. Pitchers can last for years with that type of elbow, or they could need surgery tomorrow.

The Indians claim they never said this, but one member of the front office, a baseball person, compared Jerrod Riggan to Paul Shuey. He meant that Riggan had that kind of stuff, and Charlie Manuel also heard the same thing. The baseball person was operating off someone's faulty scouting report, which became obvious once anyone saw Riggan and how his stuff was barely average.

Shapiro later admitted that Riggan was the "last piece of the deal, without him, we would not have made it." So obviously, someone, for some reason, was high on the right-hander who faded so quickly.

What no one in the Tribe front office was willing to say about the Alomar trade is now painfully obvious. The process was sabotaged by rookie mistakes, a lack of planning, and excess optimism despite data on players [especially Escobar] that should have served as caution flags, if not outright deal breakers.

"We'd deal Alomar again," said Antonetti. "But we'd do it to get the best possible prospects. We'd look deeper into their farm system, not just at the Class AAA level. Back then we wanted guys who could help us *now*, because we thought we could contend. Our goal should have been to get the best possible prospects at any level."

Shapiro and Antonetti admitted they should have pushed

harder to have the deal include Jose Reyes, who became a star a few years later.

"He was in Class A, and we had only one second-hand report from a manager in that league," said Antonetti. "If this was today, we'd have two scouts who would have seen him in addition to the manager's report. We also would have better reports on the players' medical conditions."

"Our process was flawed," said Shapiro. "We should have done more research and background in multiple ways. The key is, we critically evaluated and looked at our process and realized that we had to make decisions differently. We now get about five pages on each player [being considered for a trade]. We have everything from scouting reports to statistical analysis, both traditional and creative. We have reports about a player's makeup, personality, medical history, and background. We take a look at where the player will be in two years in terms of contract situations. After this trade, we immediately changed how we do business."

CHAPTER 5

"FREE-AGENT FASCINATION"

WHERE DID ALL THE PROSPECTS GO?

There was a time when the Indians had perhaps the best scouting and farm system in baseball. They developed three Hall of Fame–caliber hitters in Jim Thome, Albert Belle, and Manny Ramirez. Add in these names: Richie Sexson, Brian Giles, and Sean Casey, who became All-Stars with other teams.

Pitchers?

Charles Nagy, Danny Graves, Steve Kline, Chad Ogea, Paul Shuey, Bartolo Colon, and Jaret Wright all had solid to strong careers. All of those players were signed between 1988 and 1994. It's amazing testimony to the approach to signing and developing young players first put into place by former general manager Hank Peters, then continued by John Hart.

But after the Indians appeared in the 1995 World Series, something changed. The new prospects stopped coming. The maturing prospects were often traded. The Indians became a franchise solely focused on winning today, and they nearly sold out their tomorrow. They stopped paying as much attention to scouting and the farm system.

When Mark Shapiro began trading veterans for young players, he talked about how the Indians were paying for some deals designed to get them back to the World Series. Hardcore Tribe fans know which ones:

• Danny Graves, Damian Jackson, Scott Winchester, and Jim Crowell to the Reds for Jeff Branson and John Smiley on July 31, 1997. That deal became a disaster. Smiley pitched 37 innings for the Tribe, then broke his arm *while warming up in the bullpen.* He never appeared in a big league game. Graves went on to save 182 games for the Reds. Jackson has had a long career as a utility player.

• Steve Kline to Montreal for Jeff Juden on July 31, 1997. Yes, the same day as the Danny Graves trade. The Indians gave up Graves and Kline, two guys good enough to anchor the bullpen for years. In return, they received two starting pitchers who were 2-5, pitched 67 forgettable innings, and were gone within six months. Kline was traded in his rookie season. He want on to pitch for nine years and was an excellent lefty reliever. His career ERA is 3.53. He had seven consecutive seasons of ERAs under 3.75 and an ERA of 0.96 in 13 postseason games.

• Sean Casey to the Reds for Dave Burba on March 30, 1998. Burba had some solid seasons for the Indians. From 1998 to 2001, Burba was 56–35 and rarely missed a start. Casey became a .300 hitter for the Reds.

• Brian Giles to Pittsburgh for Ricky Rincon on November 18, 1998. Giles became a star outfielder for the Pirates, Rincon was a situational left-handed reliever who had arm problems with the Tribe.

• Richie Sexson, Kane Davis, Paul Rigdon, and Marco Scutaro to Milwaukee for Bob Wickman, Jason Bere, and Steve Woodard on July 28, 2000. Bere and Woodard did little. Wickman has become one of the best closers in Tribe history. Sexson matured into one of the game's premier power hitters.

Belle, Thome, and Ramirez left via free agency.

"Think about the players," said Shapiro. "We produced so many great hitters—Sexson, Giles, Casey, Ramirez, Belle, and Thome. When you lose those guys, you just don't replace them."

Shapiro was working in the Tribe farm system when the trades involving Casey, Kline, Graves, and Giles were made. He was assistant general manager at the time of Sexson deal.

"You have to remember what was going on," said Shapiro. "We believed we were so close to a title. We wanted to get back to the World Series. When you transition to a contending team, then your prospects often are used in trades to bring you immediate help."

Shapiro especially regrets the Casey and Graves deals because he believes that he could have taken a stronger stand to keep them. As farm director, he knew both players very well.

"They are two of the finer guys I've met in the game, and they had all the attributes that I recognized at a gut level would make them special," he said. "But I also knew it was hard to detach myself emotionally from them. I wondered if I was overvaluing them. The groundswell of scouting evaluations was not that strong. None of the reports were negative, but it was way underevaluating them. Especially in terms of their makeup, which separates those two guys."

The front office also was so blinded by the quest to win now that it ignored the performance of Casey and Graves.

Graves had been the Indians Minor League Pitcher of the Year for two seasons in a row—1995 and 1996. His career minor league totals were 8-4 with 50 saves and a 1.08 ERA. That's not a misprint, his ERA was 1.08. But he was a sinker ball pitcher with a soft, five-foot-eleven, 200-pound body. His fastball was average at best. He didn't impress, he just achieved. Hart also preferred hard throwers in the bullpen. Think of Jose Mesa, Eric Plunk, Steve Karsay, and Danys Baez. Guys whose fastball lit up the radar gun and awed scouts. Manager Mike Hargrove had a 30-inning audition with Graves in 1997 (2-0, 4.55 ERA) and was not overwhelmed. Many in the front office wondered if Graves threw hard enough to be a consistent closer. The Indians needed a starting pitcher, and Smiley was a journeyman lefty who had won 100 big league games—so who cared about Graves? Give us Smiley now and we'll worry about the future later.

At the time of the trade, Casey was twenty-three and had a career minor league average of .348! In 1997, he began the year hitting .386 at Class AA Akron, then advanced to Class AAA Buffalo, where he batted .361. Some of the Indians brass thought he lacked power to be a traditional first baseman. He had only 15 homers in 1997. They also had Jim Thome, newly moved to first base.

I remember Charlie Manuel dismissing Casey. In 1998, Manuel was the team's hitting coach and a confidant of Hart. Manuel told me he thought Casey would have problems in the big leagues. At best he'd be an average hitter without much power. Normally an astute judge of hitters, Manuel insisted Casey had a "chicken wing swing," a strange uppercut that would prevent him from being a consistent run producer. He saw Casey as a slow, singles-hitting first baseman. I argued with Manuel for a while, because I had seen Casey constantly hitting line drives in Akron. When the trade was announced, I wrote in a column that the Indians would regret the deal years later. Reds general manager Jim Bowden carried the story around for months, showing it to friends, fans, and media members.

But in the spring of 1998, the Indians weren't thinking about the future. They had just lost to Florida in Game 7 of the 1997 World Series, and all efforts were focused on returning to the playoffs. World Series dreams danced in their heads and clouded their thinking. Hart often talked to me about "the window of opportunity." He correctly asserted it wouldn't be open forever. By 1998, I also had a feeling Hart would not be around forever, either. He'd talk privately about how it was more fun to build a team than to try and keep contending. He believed fan and media expectations in Cleveland had become unrealistic after the Indians went to the World Series in 1995 and 1997. He feared the big-budget Yankees and Boston.

As one member of the Tribe front office told me, "John used to be very engaged in the minor league system. He really lived the player development end of it. But once we started winning, he didn't pay as much attention. He was fixated on the big league club. We all got what I call 'free-agent fascination.' We became consumed with other teams' players—from Dave Burba to David Justice to Wil Cordero. We overrated them and underrated our own players. That's a trap, because you can see the flaws in your own players easier, you are around them more often. You often don't see the weaknesses in the other team's players because you don't see them regularly."

Even in a "gotta win now" frenzy, the Giles/Rincon trade defied any sense of logic.

Brian Giles had been a backup outfielder with the Tribe in 1997, hitting .268 with 17 homers and 68 RBI in 377 at-bats. He was twenty-seven years old. Just as the Indians loved hard-throwing pitchers, they were enamored with power-hitting outfielders. They ignored the fact that Giles was a career .307 hitter in the minors and focused on him never hitting more than 20 homers in any pro season. After the 1997 season, they had brought back Kenny Lofton as a free agent, and he joined David Justice and Manny Ramirez in the projected 1998 outfield. Where would Giles fit in?

They were desperate for a lefty reliever. Hart was convinced that having two effective lefties in the bullpen was the key to beating the Yankees in a playoff series, and he wanted someone to help Paul Assenmacher. Pittsburgh came calling with Ricardo Rincon, who was 0–2 with a 2.91 ERA. At the time of the deal, Rincon was twenty-eight years old. Most of his experience was in the Mexican League. He had thrown only 125 big league innings with a 4–10 record and 3.17 ERA. He was never going to be anything more than a specialist. Giles had a chance to be an effective big league outfielder who hit all kinds of pitching reasonably well and could play all three outfield positions. The Indians didn't care, they needed a lefty reliever—right now! So they made the deal.

That's when the Indians really hit bottom. They lost their soul because they entirely ignored what had made them a contender. Perhaps trading Giles made some sense, but for a lefty who pitches to one or two batters a game? A lefty who could help them beat the Yankees? Giving up an outfielder when you didn't need to be Branch Rickey or even John Hart to know the crop was getting very thin in the minors? If Hart hadn't traded Kline for Juden, he never would have been in this situation. Kline would have been his second lefty reliever. Kline was two years younger than Rincon and a much better pitcher. Both were rookies in 1997. The Pirates were patient with Rincon, the Indians gave up on Kline quickly.

Between July 31, 1997, and November 18, 1998—a period of less than sixteen months—the Indians traded four players who would become All-Stars: Casey, Graves, Giles, and Sexson.

In return, only Wickman became an All-Star. (That happened in 2005.)

"Very few farm systems could survive that," said Shapiro. "And we had some bad drafts."

Bad is putting it mildly.

Consider the impact players the Indians drafted in the late 1980s and early 1990s. The following became All-Stars somewhere: Belle, Nagy, Thome, Giles, Ramirez, Sexson, Colon, and Graves. Several others have had solid big league careers.

Here are the Indians' top amateur draft picks from 1987 to 1995, along with some important Latin American amateur signings:

1987: No first-round pick. Albert Belle, 2nd round; Steve Olin, 16th
round.

1988: Mark Lewis and Charles Nagy, both 1st round.

1989: Calvin Murray, 1st round (didn't sign). Alan Embree, 5th round;
Jim Thome, 13th round; Brian Giles, 17th round.

1990: Tim Costo, 1st round. David Bell, 7th round. Julian Tavarez and
Einar Diaz signed as Latin American free agents.

1991: Manny Ramirez, 1st round. Herbert Perry, 2nd round; Chad
Ogea, 3rd round; Paul Byrd, 4th round; Albie Lopez, 20th round;
Damian Jackson, 44th round.

1992: Paul Shuey, 1st round.

1993: Daron Kirkreit, 1st round. Steve Kline, 8th round; Richie Sexson,
24th round. Bartolo Colon signed as a Latin American free agent.

1994: Jaret Wright, 1st round. Danny Graves, 4th round; Russell Branyan, 7th round.

1995: David Miller, 1st round. Sean Casey, 2nd round.

When you consider that list, virtually every draft was producing at least one very useful player.

Here are the top picks from 1996 to 2000:

1996: Danny Peoples, 1st round. Only John McDonald (12th round)
and David Riske (56th round) were of any significance. Best
move was signing Victor Martinez as a Latin American free agent.

1997: Tim Drew, 1st round. Only Dustin Mohr (9th round) had any
time in the majors, and he made it with the Twins as a backup
outfielder.

1998: C.C. Sabathia, 1st round. Ryan Drese (5th round) has been a
so-so starting pitcher with the Tribe, Texas, and Washington.

1999: No first-rounder. Wil Hartley, 2nd round. Fernando Cabrera (10th
round) and Jason Davis (21st round) have shown some promise
with the Tribe. Best move was signing Jhonny Peralta as a Latin
American free agent.

2000: Corey Smith, 1st round. Brian Tallet (2nd round) showed some promise, but had arm problems. Ryan Church (14th round) has become a backup outfielder with Washington.

While the Indians had seven All-Stars from 1988 to 1995, only Sabathia and Martinez have been All-Stars since. There haven't even been many decent big league backups. Of the five first-rounders from 1996 to 2000, only Sabathia has played a full season in the majors. That's awful, as more than 50 percent of first-rounders do make the big leagues.

From 1996 to 2000, the Indians had three scouting directors in five years. The turnover was devastating because when a director leaves, sometimes scouts do, too. The scouting department also lost its focus on the kind of players who needed to be drafted. There was no consistent form of evaluation.

"We were winning, so we picked lower in the draft," said Shapiro. "That's also a factor. And we signed some major league free agents, which meant we lost Number 1 picks as compensation. In 1999, our first pick wasn't until Number 74."

That was Wil Hartley, a catcher who was hurt and never even reached Class AA.

There is much validity to Shapiro's insistence that the lack of first-rounders hurt. *Baseball Prospectus* has done extensive studies on the draft and discovered that nearly 50 percent of the top 100 picks in each draft from 1984 to 1999 reached the majors. The first thirty-five picks (first rounds) are twice as likely to make it as the next fifty picks. It continues to drop after that. As the magazine's Rany Jazayerli wrote, "There is surprisingly little difference between second and third round draft picks."

His research revealed that first-rounders are at least twice as likely to have a significant big league career as players picked in the second and third rounds. Top 10 picks had a much higher success ratio than players picked in the rest of the first round. So the Indians did pay for their success with lower picks, lowering their odds of finding talent.

But if you study those drafts from the late 1980s through 1995, the scouts discovered gems in the low rounds, such as Thome (13th), Giles (17th), and Sexson (24th). That stopped happening after 1995. The turmoil on the scouting staff has to be the reason. When Shapiro became general manager after the 2001 season, one of his first moves was to promote John Mirabelli from a regular scout to scouting director, a position he still held heading into the 2006 season. It's too early to evaluate his drafts—it takes four to five years for most players to make the majors, and another two to three years for them to reveal what type of impact they'll make. But the Indians gained some stability. They also poured real money into scouting and player development. From 2002 to 2005, they ranked in the top three in spending on scouting and the minor league system. That was a priority set by the Dolans. Before that, the Indians were in the middle of the major league pack during the late 1990s.

As Paul Dolan mentioned, "This is not like being Number 1 in payroll, because the difference isn't huge. We'll spend about $25 million. The average team is about $18 million a year."

But that extra $7 million should pay for better scouts, better instructors, and better bonuses for drafted players, as well as Latin American scouting and player development. This is very wise spending.

But for most of the 2000s, the Indians paid a heavy price for contention in the 1990s.

"Had they kept Casey, Giles, Graves, and Sexson, they'd have been in super shape," said Tribe broadcaster Tom Hamilton. "That's where not winning a World Series forced them to make deals that came back to haunt the organization. There was the sense that 'We've got to win a World Series now!' They kept making trades for what they thought was that one missing piece. They kept worrying about the window of opportunity closing. What happened was that we got old all at once, and we didn't have the energy that young guys bring to a club. I kept thinking that if we had won the 1997 World Series, we'd still have Brian Giles in our outfield."

Assistant general manager Chris Antonetti has studied what happened to the Indians and to contending teams in general. When you stop producing young players and infusing them into your team, you eventually run into trouble.

"Players tend to get better from their early to middle twenties, that's when they show the most growth," he explained. "They peak in their late twenties and early thirties, then they begin to decline. But what also happens is their salaries go up. They get hurt more often. That happened to us and we didn't have the players to replace them. That's why we had to make the moves we did—like the Colon trade."

CHAPTER 6

"WE'RE BUYING PROSPECTS."

REALITY ARRIVES, BARTOLO COLON GOES

Mark Shapiro and his staff knew that trading Roberto Alomar was just the first move in trying to revive the Tribe. Shapiro and his two assistant general managers, Chris Antonetti and Neal Huntington, began a serious study of how teams were rebuilt. They discovered there were three roads:

- Spend a lot of money on major league free agents. This was not going to happen, because attendance was dropping and the payroll was being cut.
- Promote young players from the farm system. That wasn't going to happen, either. There just wasn't enough talent, especially at the upper minor league levels.
- Acquire prospects from other teams, using established major leaguers in trades to do it. This was the only viable alternative, and they'd already started on it, to an extent, with the Alomar deal. But Shapiro knew they had to do more—and, yes, do better.

Antonetti did some research that made it more apparent that the Indians could not just wait for the players they were drafting and signing to develop. The Indians had to get some good young players, and get them now.

"It takes four to five years after you sign guys for most of them to make the majors, assuming they even do make it," Antonetti said. "And after they're in the majors, it's another three years at least for them to really develop. So you are talking at least seven years from the time most players are signed for them to become viable big league players. In some cases, it's as much as nine years."

Antonetti rolled out some other numbers:

• In 1992 the Oakland A's won 96 games. They didn't have another winning season until 1999. In 2000, they made the playoffs. It took them seven years to return to contention.

• In 1992 the Minnesota Twins were 90–72. They didn't have another winning season until 2001. In 2002, they made the playoffs. It took them nine years to contend again.

• In 1992 the Pittsburgh Pirates won their division. They have not had a winning record since.

• The Kansas City Royals have not been series contenders in more than a decade.

• The Detroit Tigers have not had a winning season since 1993.

There were more examples, but the pattern was obvious and disturbing.

"If we just waited, let our veterans become free agents, really concentrated on drafting and developing even better than ever, we were looking at seven or more years to really rebuild," said Antonetti.

Left unsaid was that none of the current front office would be around to see it, assuming it happened at all. There are no guarantees. Look at the struggles in Detroit, Milwaukee, Kansas City, Pittsburgh, and to a lesser extent, Cincinnati. Those teams seem to have been on different rebuilding plans for more than a decade. That's because only 8 to 12 percent of all players signed have any sort of significant major league career. The development game was stacked against the Indians.

When Mark Shapiro looked at his 2001 Class AAA Buffalo roster, the best position players were Milton Bradley, Karim Garcia, John McDonald, and Tim Laker. Only Bradley had star potential.

The top pitchers were Tim Drew and Jake Westbrook. The best player in the minors was Victor Martinez, a switch-hitting catcher who had just won the 2001 Class A Carolina League batting title. But he was probably three years away from starting for the Tribe, assuming he continued to mature at his current rate.

"From Day One of spring training, I was thinking about the time when we'd have to completely retool," said Shapiro. "We assigned our scouts to check out the top prospects in several organizations, so that we would be ready to move if the time came and we didn't contend as I hoped."

Scouting would be a vital part of the solution.

"We improved our minor league scouting staff," said Antonetti. "Traditionally, that job was an afterthought. There are big league scouts, which are primarily advance scouts [who put together reports on the teams you play next or players for whom you may trade]. There also are amateur league scouts. But the players in the middle—the minor leagues—weren't being heavily scouted. Knowing that this [finding talent from other franchises' minor league teams] was going to be a lifeblood for us, we invested heavily. We brought in more scouts, and scouts whom we thought could make an impact."

This was discussed in the final years of the John Hart regime, but it wasn't fully implemented until the spring of 2002. Once again during this period, the perception that the Dolans were cutting financial corners was a fallacy. In 1999, they spent $16 million on their scouting and farm system, which ranked in the middle of the major league pack. By 2002, it was up to $24 million, among the top three in baseball. That investment was about to pay off in the Bartolo Colon deal.

The Indians examined other organizations, asking themselves "Who would most want Bartolo Colon, and who would have the most prospects to trade?" They came up with five teams: the Yankees, the Braves, the Reds, the Rangers, and the Expos. The first four were contenders, or at least thought they should contend. Montreal made the list simply because the Expos had lots of prospects.

Next they assembled a list of prospects who were of interest. The top five were: Adam Dunn (Reds); Austin Kearns (Reds); Hank Blaylock (Rangers); Nick Johnson (Yankees); Brandon Phillips (Expos).

The list had far more names, but they wanted to trade for at least one player among their top five.

The Indians certainly didn't advertise they were considering trading Colon. He was twenty-nine years old, and his fastball sometimes peaked at 100 mph. He seemed to throw harder in the eighth inning than the first. He was a bull of man at six feet, 240 pounds. He'd always have issues with his weight. He'd sometimes lose concentration and confidence. Many fans were frustrated with him, believing he should be close to a 20-game winner every year, a true ace. Colon wasn't quite great, but he was very, very good. From 1998 to 2001, he won 14, 18, 15, and 14 games. He averaged 205 innings a season and eight strikeouts per nine innings.

The Indians signed and developed two talented starting pitchers in the 1990s. The first was Jaret Wright, whose career was sidetracked by shoulder problems. The other was Colon. Who knew when they'd find another Colon? To the average baseball fan, talking about dealing Colon early in the 2002 season was insanity. Weren't the Indians supposed to be building with pitching? Wasn't Colon their best pitcher? Wasn't the team supposed to contend?

"To really start the rebuilding process, that meant being prepared to trade our best players," said Shapiro. "We had to do what we did with Robbie Alomar, only be more decisive. We had to get the best prospects. We had to be prepared with our scouts having good reports and lots of looks at the best prospects available.

And we had to be willing to trade Colon, because he was our best player and would bring the most in return."

Shapiro knew Colon was signed through 2003, so that would make him attractive to other teams. They would not be trading their top prospects for a guy who could leave at the end of the year as a free agent.

Just as important, Colon would be a free agent in 2003 if the Indians kept him. Attendance was dropping, there would be no money to sign Colon to the lucrative contract he was destined to receive. Not if they wanted to add enough talent around him to contend.

The question was, which was the fastest way for the Tribe to make Colon the catalyst to spark the rebuilding process and get the Indians back into contention faster: invest heavily in him with a contract extension, or trade him? No doubt, trading Colon would bring the most prospects. The Indians also made plans to deal Chuck Finley, Paul Shuey, and any other veteran who might be of interest to another team. Anyone, that is, except Jim Thome. He would be a free agent at the end of 2002, and Shapiro hoped to re-sign him. That was another reason for trading Colon: there was no way the Indians could afford Thome and Colon. At least that was the assessment in the spring of 2002.

Then the Indians bolted to an 11–1 start. Part of Shapiro hoped this was real, that maybe the team indeed had one more Central Division title left in it. But the other part of Shapiro knew better. This was fool's gold.

"It just didn't look right to me how we were doing it," said Shapiro. "We were lucky in some of those early games. It was great that we were winning. At this point, Minnesota had not yet emerged as the team they'd become."

He kept his scouts on the road, checking out minor league prospects. Assistant general managers Antonetti and Huntington looked at a couple of big deals made by Seattle when it was obvious the Mariners could not afford to keep their stars. They traded Ken Griffey to Cincinnati, Randy Johnson to Houston. In both cases, they received significant prospects and continued to win for a few years without those players.

Meanwhile, the Dolans were thrilled with the hot start because it took the heat off them for failing to sign Ramirez and for trading Alomar.

"Early in the season, I was at the Convention Center for a charity fundraiser and Drew Carey was the host," said Paul Dolan. "The buzz was about the Indians, and Carey was calling Mark Shapiro 'the new god of Cleveland.' The next day, our game against Kansas City was rained out. Then we lost six in a row."

The team was breaking down. Travis Fryman had back problems. Bradley had various injuries. Lawton injured his shoulder. Einar Diaz didn't hit. Neither did Russell Branyan.

By May, what Shapiro and his staff had first realized after the 2001 season was confirmed—the era of the Indians owning the Central Division was over. The crowds were dwindling, as this season was no sellout. The home opener was, but in the rest of April they averaged slightly more than 25,000 fans—17,000 under capacity. Carrying a 13–13 record into May didn't exactly inspire confidence that the fans would embrace this team. They could be headed into a major fall. Then Shapiro went to the Dolans and outlined his plan to trade Colon for prospects—and then deal other veterans. It was a gutsy strategy, one that was certain to bring ownership and Shapiro an immediate and ugly backlash from fans and the media. It ran counter to what most baseball executives do, which is play it safe and try to keep their jobs as long as possible.

"We could have just stayed with our veterans and maybe won 85 games, if everything went okay," Shapiro said. "No one would have criticized us. We could have just waited for everyone to really see we needed to rebuild. Maybe that wouldn't have come until 2004—and then it would have taken eight to ten years to get back into contention."

Since the Indians ended the 2002 season without the likes of Colon, Finley, and Shuey and still were 74–88, it's possible that Shapiro's projection of 85 victories would have been correct had the team remained together. But Shapiro was not going to make the same mistake he did in the Alomar deal. He was not going to deny what his heart and head were telling him. He was going to lead the team his way, and accept the criticism and consequences. He was going to trade Bartolo Colon, trade a pitcher in his prime who seemed on his way to a 20-win season, for a bunch of players that most fans had never heard of. He was about to become the most despised man in Cleveland, or at least share that distinction with the Dolans.

"Mark was preparing us for the fact we weren't going to get a major league–ready All-Star in return for Colon," said Paul Dolan. "I originally thought we'd get a young big leaguer in return, a guy like [Montreal second baseman] Jose Vidro. I spent the next month or so with Mark nearly every day discussing the options."

Few owners would have embraced this idea. It was going to make an already sad public relations situation even more alarming. Attendance would continue to fall, and with it, revenue. They also were trusting a rookie general manager to trade away their best player. At the very least, they could have asked Shapiro to wait until the end of the year, hoping the team would rebound and somehow contend. In May and early June, the Indians usually were within five games of first-place Minnesota. It was near enough to dream, despite the team's inability to get over .500.

But the Dolans let the baseball people make the pure baseball decisions. Shapiro and his staff said now was the time. Soon, other teams would be dumping their veteran players, and it would be harder to acquire the premier prospects. The Dolans understood and watched Shapiro move forward.

The obvious place for Colon seemed to be the Yankees. They continually traded prospects for veterans, and they never worried about the long-term impact. They had the bankroll to just keep spending for more free agents. The Indians liked minor league first baseman Nick Johnson and some other young players. But the Yankees surprised the Tribe by showing little interest in Colon. They seemed to be worried about his weight and had mixed scouting reports on him.

Shapiro liked several players with Cincinnati, and Reds general manager Jim Bowden had been a regular trading partner with John Hart. Adam Dunn and Austin Kearns both were power hitters. The Tribe also had an interest in pitcher Brandon Claussen. But Bowden was never able to get a green light on the deal from his ownership, because Colon was making $4.6 million and they'd have to take on more payroll. The Indians talked to the Mets, Rangers, and other teams, but made little progress.

Early in May, I heard the Indians were considering a trade with Colon. I had written a column saying that it would be a good idea, assuming they could make a deal much like Hart did when he shipped Joe Carter to San Diego for Carlos Baerga and Sandy Alomar. Both were Class AAA players, and Alomar had been featured in the *Sporting News* and was *Baseball America*'s Minor League Player of the Year. He seemed destined to be the Indians' starting catcher for the next ten years. Baerga wasn't as highly regarded, but there was little doubt he'd be a solid big league infielder. Another example was when the Indians shipped Sean Casey to the Reds for veteran pitcher Dave Burba. Casey was one of the top hitters in all of the minors, and he was big league ready. I suggested the Indians should be able to get a Casey and more prospects for Colon, who clearly was a better pitcher than Burba.

In late May, Shapiro called Montreal general manager Omar Minaya. The Expos were shocking contenders in the National

League East. They were in a strange situation. The team was owned by Major League Baseball, which was trying to find an ownership group in another city so the Expos could move. Minaya was hired by Major League Baseball to run the franchise until a buyer could be found. He had no idea if he'd have a job the following year. There was no reason for him to worry about long-term prospects. If he could somehow acquire a player to help his team make the playoffs now, Major League Baseball would be thrilled, because it would make the franchise more attractive to possible buyers. Minaya also would look great, and possibly remain as general manager when the team moved—or be hired by another team.

"I love Colon, I really do," Minaya told Shapiro. "I have prospects to trade you. But I'm owned by Major League Baseball, and I can't take on his salary."

Shapiro really wanted to make a deal with Montreal because he had better information on their prospects than those from other teams, and not just because his two assistant general managers, Antonetti and Huntington, had worked for the Expos. The Indians had also hired Tony LaCava, formerly the Expos' minor league director. They had been scouting the Expos' farm teams intensely.

Shapiro knew he had to make this trade, and he knew his best chance was with the Expos. He correctly believed his strength was his ability to bring together scouting reports, medical reports, assessments of a player's attitude and personality, and statistical data—and from all that, form a picture of the player. John Hart could watch a player a few times and just "know" if that prospect had the right stuff because Hart himself had played and managed in the minors. Shapiro didn't have that advantage. For his decisions he used his Princeton education and his experience being around baseball people of all types—from the old school that used the eyes and instinct, like Hart, to the new one based on statistics and other data, pioneered by Oakland's Billy

Beane and the Moneyball school of executives. Shapiro is smart enough to know what he doesn't know and humble enough not to fully marry into any one philosophy of scouting players. The Moneyball types care only about statistics and would scoff if they heard an old-line baseball man such as Buddy Bell say, "I really like Coco Crisp's swing. I think he'll hit .300. You can't throw a fastball past that little guy." But Shapiro would hear that—in fact, it's exactly what he heard from Bell in the spring of 2004. Buddy Bell rarely raves about young players. He has seen decades of baseball. If Buddy Bell likes a player's swing, you'd better pay attention—no matter what the statistics may say. In the case of Crisp, there were some numbers to back up Bell. But Bell's words were stronger than the statistics, and Bell's words turned out to be gospel. You can't consistently throw a fastball past Crisp, even if it's 100 mph. And he did hit .300 in 2005.

Shapiro knew something else: prospects are just that—prospects. Most won't make it. Most who do reach the majors don't play up to expectations. It isn't quite like buying a lottery ticket in hopes of paying the mortgage, but there are no sure things in this game. Prospects often are like tech stocks. Somewhere is the next Google, the next Amazon.com, the next eBay. But there also are so many names that will barely be answers to trivia questions a few years from now.

Montreal . . .

Yes, Montreal was the team.

Somehow they had to make a deal with Montreal.

Shapiro has a method he calls "blue-skying it," a form of brainstorming with his advisors. How could they make the trade if Montreal couldn't pay Colon? Someone in the room asked, "What if we take on the money?" Meaning, what if the Indians paid Colon's salary? Or what if they found a player on Montreal's roster who made as much as Colon and added that guy to the deal? Trading salary for salary. They found a guy, veteran first baseman Lee Stevens, who was at the end of his career. Shapiro ran the idea past Paul Dolan.

Many owners would have said, "Wait a minute, we're going to trade our best pitcher for a bunch of kids, and we don't know if they'll make it. We're going to get killed in the media—again. The fans are going to scream. We're only five games out of first place, and it's going to look like we're writing off the season. And we gotta pay Colon, too?"

No doubt, part of Paul Dolan wanted to say that.

"I had spent more than a month with Mark on this process," he said. "He did not have to sell us on the idea of trading Colon. We were totally on board. Mark had some concerns about signing Colon to a big extension. He had some health concerns [weight] about Bartolo. But the main point was that Bartolo could bring us what we needed in terms of prospects."

Shapiro explained, "We're buying prospects. We are artificially creating [amateur] drafts, and we're paying for the prospects. Taking back Colon's salary is kind of like giving these guys signing bonuses, had they been in the draft."

"I knew our plan was right, and if paying the salary was what we needed to do, then we'd do it," said Paul Dolan. "My main concern was [that] we got the right guys for Colon. I sat in most of those meetings as they talked about the various prospects, but I didn't know these players. I knew what our organization thought of the various prospects, but I didn't know if they were the right guys. I wanted to help Mark do what was necessary to make sure we got the best guys."

Shapiro was convinced those guys were with Montreal, so the Dolans approved picking up the salary. They later would do the same when Chuck Finley was traded to St. Louis and Paul Shuey to the Dodgers. The Dolans wisely believed it was worth the investment on their end to give Shapiro the dollar power to make the best deal.

This was late June. The trading deadline was at the end of July. Usually, teams start unloading their veterans in the hope of dumping big contracts and picking up prospects after the All-Star game in the middle of July. Shapiro wanted to get to the best prospects first. He also knew that, although Montreal was within four games of first place now, they could easily have a bad week and suddenly slip to seven games behind. What then? They might not want to trade their prospects, after all.

In the final week of June, everything told Shapiro he had to make this deal *now.*

Shapiro asked about young second baseman Jose Vidro, knowing the Expos would probably not part with him, which was true. He pushed for outfielder Brad Wilkerson, who would be the ideal leadoff hitter to replace Kenny Lofton. No way, said Montreal. The Expos explained they would not part with any of their key major league players. They wanted to make a pennant run this minute. They could not afford to weaken the big league roster at any point, or why make the Colon trade? The idea wasn't just to stay even in the National League East race, it was to get better.

But the farm system . . .

The farm system was deep and rich . . .

The farm system was open for business . . .

When Shapiro opened serious trade talks with the Expos, they were three games out of first place. Then four games. Then five games.

Brandon Phillips was ranked the number-one prospect in the Expos farm system by *Baseball America* and nearly everyone else. The Indians had seen him seven different times, with five scouts doing the evaluating. Here are the basics they reported:

• A candidate to become an All-Star shortstop in the majors

• A terrific athlete with an above-average arm and hands and excellent range

• An above-average bat, especially for a middle infielder

He was twenty years old, playing at Class AA Harrisburg and batting .327 with nine homers and 35 RBI in 245 at-bats. He was about to be promoted to Class AAA.

The Tribe's consensus scouting report read:

> Exciting young player . . . Aggressive hitter with bat speed and reactions at plate, makes hard contact . . . Hammers mistakes . . . Drives ball well to all fields with pull homerun power . . . Has body to add strength and maturity, which will only improve his power . . . Defensively, has the hands, actions and arm to play SS . . . Flashy defender capable of spectacular plays. Bat should be enough for middle of the lineup. All-Star potential.

"Everyone thought he'd be an above-average hitter and an impact player," said Shapiro. "We had excellent reports on him going back to 1999, when he was an amateur. He was the cornerstone guy, the first one we asked for."

Phillips was such a gifted athlete that he had a scholarship offer to play point guard for the University of Georgia, but the five-foot-eleven, 190-pounder signed with the Expos after being drafted in the second round.

Looking at all this now, you might ask yourself, "What happened to Phillips?"

Granted, he'll only turn twenty-five during the 2006 season, but he has yet to establish himself as a major leaguer. He failed in several trials with the Indians, and the longer he's played in the minors, the more he's struggled to hit. Shapiro began his baseball career as a minor league administrator, so he knew that even "can't miss" players do just that. He was not about to bet the near future of the franchise on just one prospect, no matter how highly he was regarded.

The next Expos prospect on the Indians' list was twenty-three-year-old Cliff Lee, and these were the basics:

- Left-handed pitcher with above-average control, above-average fastball, above-average breaking pitches.
- Not afraid to pitch inside.
- Made hitters swing and miss, had 297 strikeouts in 240 innings compared to only 105 walks in his minor league career.
- Only twenty-three years old, was 7–2 with a 3.23 ERA and 105 strikeouts in 86 innings at Class AA Harrisburg.
- Could be a number two or number three starter in the majors.
- Could get to the big leagues soon, a rarity because of being left-handed and having good control.
- Could be a major league pitcher in the Chuck Finley mode.

The Tribe's consensus scouting report read:

> Lefthanded starter . . . average to above average on four pitches. Could compete at the Major League level right now. He still needs to work on consistency with his curve and changeup . . . Strikeout pitcher using his fastball with life and deception . . . True slider with sharp, late break . . . Can throw any pitch at any time . . . Good starter on a winning team.

Everything looked good about Lee, from his numbers to his stuff. Rarely does a pitcher average more than a strikeout per inning, but Lee did. The fact that his fastball was just above the big league average of 90 mph wasn't the point. More important was that he had control of it, and he could get strikeouts. His ball had movement, sometimes sinking, sometimes sailing. A 90 mph fastball with "life" is a much better pitch than a 95 mph fastball that just comes in straight and dead.

The last prospect was Grady Sizemore, who was batting only .258 with no home runs, and 26 RBI in 75 games at Class A Brevard City. It was his third pro year; his other averages in the low minors were .293 and .268. At the time of the deal, he had a grand total of three homers in 912 at-bats.

"He was a guy we wanted in the deal from Day One," said Shapiro. "Tony LaCava had been Montreal's farm director, and then was a scout for us. He knew Grady personally. He liked him a lot. We had the same seven looks [with five scouts] at Grady as we did their other prospects. The fact that he wasn't performing real well for them didn't bother me, because he was only nineteen."

Shapiro's director of player personnel, Steve Lubratich, played seven years of pro ball (including 64 games in the big leagues) before becoming a minor league manager, then a member of the front office in San Diego and Detroit. He is more of a pure baseball man, and his opinion really is important to Shapiro. Lubratich scouted Sizemore twice and rated him a "6," which is impressive. Players are rated 1–8 on skills on some scouting reports—any rating 6 or higher is rated as a major league–caliber player. Minor league hitting coordinator Gary Dembo was dispatched to watch Sizemore and came back raving about his swing. Former big league pitcher Tim Belcher, another Tribe advisor, scouted Sizemore and was impressed by his natural athleticism and by how he played with passion. The fact that Lubratich and some of the other scouts were so impressed by Sizemore mattered more to Shapiro than the kid's unimpressive numbers.

The basics on the nineteen-year-old Sizemore looked liked this:

- A tremendous natural athlete. He was a high school quarterback who rushed for 3,081 yards in his career and had an offer to play quarterback for the Washington Huskies. He was a three-sport high school star who ran a 4.5 in the 40-yard dash.
- A very smart kid, graduated with a 3.85 grade-point average at the age of seventeen.

- Was a third-round pick by the Expos.
- Has excellent athletic size at six feet two, 200 pounds. He's graceful and fluid.
- May not hit for power now but will, thanks to a compact left-handed swing.
- Above-average speed and range in center field. A below-average arm.
- Plays hard all the time, great attitude. A winner.
- Still raw but can mature into an impact player. One scout saw a little of Kirk Gibson in Sizemore.
- At the very least, a starting outfielder like Trot Nixon or Brad Wilkerson.

The Tribe's consensus scouting report read:

> Solid defender. Arm solid average. Accuracy and carry can improve as he lengthens his arm stroke . . . Made plays in all directions with good routes and reads to the ball, showed no fear of going into the wall . . . Professional at-bats, showed plate discipline and patience. Did not chase pitches out of the strike zone. Good balance at the plate, good 2-strike approach . . . Projects as solid Major League hitter . . . Did not show the ability to drive the ball out of the park in games or batting practice . . . Power should develop into solid average . . . Coaches rave about his work ethic . . . Should develop into a solid everyday Major League outfielder.

The Expos agreed to the prospects, and Shapiro was ready to push for a fourth prospect when Colon strained his back while pitching and left a game early. He was sent back to Cleveland for an MRI, which showed no damage. He was 10–4 with a 2.55 ERA. Shapiro knew that he really had the three key pieces to the deal, so he decided to get it done before anything else happened—a Montreal losing streak, a real injury to Colon, or the Expos just changing their minds.

On June 27, 2002, the trade was agreed upon. Colon and fading Tribe prospect Tim Drew for Lee Stevens, Sizemore, Phillips, and Lee.

It would be announced the next day.

CHAPTER 7

"FANS WERE SCREAMING AT US."

TAKING HEAT WHILE GATHERING YOUNG TALENT

So much for planning . . .

Understand that the Indians did their homework on the Bartolo Colon trade. They'd learned much in the six months since the Alomar trade. They had one goal in mind: prospects. They spent months researching the young players, using multiple scouts watching them several times. They had medical records. They had information on attitudes and family backgrounds. This was not a trade with a mixed message about rebuilding and contending. It was a trade about new beginnings, about trying to save the Tribe. It was about a unique opportunity to pick the first fruits from one of baseball's ripest farm systems. Who knew when there would ever be a team such as Montreal, owned by Major League Baseball, trying to win a playoff spot—and no one really caring about next year or the players of the future? It was a trade that had to be made, and made now for a variety of reasons.

The Indians would explain all that and more the morning after the deal was agreed upon. They planned to have quotes from *Baseball America* and other sources to show that not only did they value the prospects highly, but so did the baseball establishment. They knew this trade would be a tough sell, and they intended to sell it hard.

"I knew there would be misunderstandings," said Shapiro. "I knew our manager [Charlie Manuel] and our players would be devastated. I knew the fans and the media really wouldn't understand. I knew our front office that wasn't part of the baseball side wouldn't understand. I knew that we had to explain this with candor and consistency, and do it over and over."

The Indians were playing in Boston that evening. Colon was not with the team. He had returned to Cleveland to have his strained back examined. Shapiro called the pitcher and informed him of the deal. He wanted to make sure that Colon didn't hear it from anywhere else. Remarkably, there were no media rumors of a pending deal with Montreal. The lid had been put on and cemented shut, exactly how the Indians planned it.

So far, everything was falling into place. The Indians were able to secure the prospects they wanted. Colon's back was not a problem. Colon learned of the trade directly from Shapiro. Now the general manager planned to watch his team play that night in Boston on TV, and then hold a press conference the following morning to explain the trade to the public. Montreal also agreed to wait until the next morning for the announcement.

Then the lid blew off.

Shapiro was watching ESPN when the news line on the bottom of the screen reported: INDIANS TRADE BARTOLO COLON TO MONTREAL FOR LEE STEVENS AND THREE PROSPECTS.

Assistant general manager Chris Antonetti was with the team in the clubhouse when ESPN broke the story.

"The players were looking at Chris, wondering what was going on," said Shapiro. "The announcement on ESPN made it look like Lee Stevens was the key to the deal. He was just a way for us to make the money work on the trade. The point was the prospects, not Lee Stevens."

Suddenly, nothing was going according to plan.

"From a public relations standpoint, this was awful," said Bob DiBiasio, the Tribe's vice president of public relations. "It leaked out of Montreal. Their game was delayed by rain. They were excited about the deal. One of their front office people told their media. So we quickly threw together a phone press conference that night with Mark Shapiro and our media, and we didn't have a chance to explain what happened. It sounded like we really wanted Stevens and that we were just getting three guys, none of whom was even as high as Class AAA."

Being a sports columnist, I was on the other end of this announcement. It was about 9 p.m. when the media received word that Shapiro would soon have a telephone press conference to discuss trading Colon. The media had been given the names of the players, but they meant little at that point—and there was no time to do any real research. Shapiro began talking around 9:30 p.m. It lasted about thirty minutes. That made it 10 p.m. My story was due in an hour. There was no time to call scouts or front office people from other teams who could help me with background. Cliff Lee and Brandon Phillips had impressive numbers in Class AA, but I was hoping for at least one player with some serious Class AAA experience as part of the deal—much like when the Indians traded Joe Carter for Sandy Alomar and Carlos Baerga after the 1989 season. Phillips had just been promoted to Class AAA, been there ten days. As for Grady Sizemore, that sounded like a major gamble. He was nineteen, playing in Class A and hitting .258 with *zero* homers in 256 at-bats.

And Lee Stevens?

As Tribe public relations director Bart Swain recently described him to me, "He was an old first baseman with a bad body. We were trying to tell everyone this was not about Lee Stevens."

Especially since he was thirty-four, headed to free agency, and hitting .190.

Swain knew exactly what would happen to many of us in the media. He knew it was late at night, and stories had to be written immediately. Talk show hosts went on the air with very little information. While Shapiro tried to outline the reasoning for the trade, it was obvious that he was upset by the leak and was not as clear and persuasive as usual. Nights like that are among the few where I hate my job because I know I can't do it well. Had Colon been traded for Brad Wilkerson or some other young Montreal players plus the prospects, I could have latched on to Wilkerson. At least I knew who he was and it was obvious how he'd fit immediately with the Tribe. That story could easily have been written in an hour and been fair to all concerned.

But all there seemed to be was Lee Stevens and three kids.

My story from that night is the one I regret the most in a long career spent writing about Cleveland sports. The headline was:

COLON TRADE A SLAP IN THE FACE TO FANS
SHAPIRO TALKS ABOUT REBUILDING THE TEAM,
BUT WRECKING BALL WHISKS AWAY
TRIBE'S TOP PITCHER TO MONTREAL.

Reporters and columnists don't write the headlines on their own stories. That is done by editors at the office who receive the stories sent via computer, read them, then try to summarize the main theme in a short, provocative headline. That's why there are times when the headline just doesn't seem to match the story. The two items were written by two different people. But in this case, I can't blame the headline writer. He caught the mood of my story, which began:

Mark Shapiro had better be right because a team can only trade Bartolo Colon once. And the Tribe's general manager did just that, shipping Colon to Montreal for veteran first baseman Lee Stevens and three prospects.

This one hurts.

The Tribe has finally developed an elite starting pitcher, and now he's gone . . . Montreal pulled a trade to make a run at the pennant . . . the Indians just made the kind of deal that has haunted the penny-pinching Expos for years, moving a star approaching free agency for a bunch of kids.

For Tribe fans, this team's future is suddenly a blast from the past. Shapiro is talking about rebuilding now. And rebuilding next season. And maybe contending in 2004, or, more likely, 2005!!!

So much for that ERA OF CHAMPIONS slogan that used to appear everywhere at Jacobs Field. The Tribe has just run up the surrender flag in the lame Central Division, where they trail Minnesota by six games. Fans are outraged, and it's easy to understand why . . .

Remember when the team handed out wrist bands as a method of selling tickets to fans who couldn't get enough of the Tribe? Now, they may have to switch to handcuffs . . .

Fans will wonder about the Indians' free fall from defending Central Division champions to a team with a 36-41 record, a team that seems like it's run by a miserly old grouch who wanders through the house, shutting off all the lights and turning the heat down to 58 . . .

It's impossible to judge a trade such as this right now, but this much is obvious—all the risk has been taken on by the Tribe, which is never a good place to be.

That's a condensed version of my column the morning after the trade. As I read it more than three years later, I realized I did what is so tempting for any of us in the media to do. When we're not sure of what we should say, we hit hot buttons. The Dolans were cheap. The Indians have made lousy trades like this before. The 1970s are back and Western Civilization is about to end. I was being inconsistent, at best. I had criticized the Indians in the Alomar deal for not solely going after the best prospects available. Now they seemed to do something like that for Colon, and

I ripped them again. I knew they weren't going to contend, even with Colon. After the 11-1 start, the Indians had lost 40 of their next 65 games by the time the trade was made.

I had missed the point, and I was in a chorus of howlers. The truth was that none of us really knew what we were talking or writing about, because none of us had seen any of the prospects nor did we have access to any real research. We live in a media age that demands instant opinions, and we delivered them—regardless. Ten hours later, I had talked to some baseball people from other teams and heard raves about Phillips and strong endorsements of Lee. I heard little about Sizemore, other than "He's a gifted athlete, but who knows if he'll develop?" But I began to feel better about the deal. Shapiro had a major press conference, armed with information and a much better presentation of why the deal was made.

"We were getting calls from fans, and they were screaming at us," said DiBiasio. "We had said we were going to build a team with pitching, and we had just traded our best pitcher because we were too cheap to sign him. We were going right back to the old days before Jacobs Field and we'd never have a decent team again."

Part of being a Tribe fan is expecting the worst from your team. For longtime fans, it's remembering the old days in a huge empty stadium on Lake Erie watching the home team lose night after night with no real hope of it ever contending.

"I made the trade knowing there would be misunderstandings, and knowing that we'd be criticized," said Shapiro. "I felt a huge leadership burden. The moment I made the trade, I knew that was I letting down multiple constituencies because most of the people you deal with as a GM are concerned only with the moment right now, and winning right now. Intellectually, I knew it was the right decision. It was the only way back. Right after the deal was announced [Reds GM] Jim Bowden told me that Phillips was a better player than anyone he had in his farm system, and they had some very good prospects. I heard things like that from a lot of baseball people. But I knew from the fans and media, not many people were going to like it."

Then Shapiro did something that was astonishing because it was so honest and so bold and could have come back to haunt him for the rest of his career. On the night of the deal, he said: "We are clearly moving in a rebuilding process aimed at 2004 and 2005. We had to consider players who could bring back multiple pieces [in a trade] so we can contend in that time frame."

The next day, he again mentioned 2004 as a possible contending season, but seemed to stress that 2005 was the real target date.

Remember, Shapiro said that on June 27, 2002.

That was like telling the fans, "We'll see you in three years." Suddenly, anyone trying to sell Tribe tickets for the rest of 2002, all of 2003, and possibly 2004 was probably going to be down on their knees and lighting holy candles, praying for a miracle. Exactly how were they supposed to market a team that had just won six Central Division titles in seven years, and now said it might be three years before they could contend again? No one had a real answer, because there was none.

Or as Tom Hamilton said, "I heard that talk of 2005 and I immediately thought I was sure glad that I wasn't in charge of ticket sales! I remember thinking, 'I don't know if I'd be that honest.' But that's Mark, he's very honest. He was going to be realistic with people and not be like some GMs who say their team will contend next year when they know it will never happen."

"It's part of my job to manage expectations," said Shapiro. "I was trying to set a realistic time frame, and people were up in arms that it would take that long. But even 2005 was really ambitious when you consider so many teams need seven to nine years to rebuild. Some teams needed twelve years, and I said we were going to do it in three. It was a big mistake to talk about contending in 2005. It hung on me like when the first George Bush said there would be no new taxes."

The Dolans weren't thrilled with Shapiro's "contend in 2005" prediction, but they accepted it with surprising calm and a little admiration.

"It was a mistake, but Mark was just expressing what he believed," said Paul Dolan. "Besides, it's out there. I mean, we were rebuilding. That's obvious. We had to acknowledge that. But to guess when we would contend again, that bothered me some because I wanted it to be before 2005. Later, I realized Mark put himself on an extraordinary timetable to turn over the roster and build a contender."

Shapiro's statement put pressure on both ends of the franchise—the business side and the baseball side. The business people suddenly knew what it had been like to sell and market the Cleveland Cavaliers before LeBron James arrived. The Cavs front office continually heard from fans who were upset about the team moving from the Richfield Coliseum to the Gund Arena in downtown Cleveland. They heard from fans who missed the Cavs teams of Mark Price, Brad Daugherty, Larry Nance, Craig Ehlo, and Lenny Wilkens. They heard from fans who were still mad about the Ron Harper trade of 1989—and that had been more than ten years ago.

Like most organizations, the Indians raised prices, sometimes severely, when the team was winning and the tickets were selling. Fans bought, but didn't like it—and expected big wins for their money. Many fans had purchased season tickets in 2002 still expecting to see a contender, which was what the front office had promised. Now, it was 1992 all over again, assuming Shapiro was correct and contention was indeed three years away.

So the business people didn't appreciate Shapiro's prediction of a three-year wait. That seemed like thirty years to them.

To the baseball people, it felt like thirty days.

Here's the 2002 opening day lineup, with the players' ages:

Matt Lawton RF (30)
Omar Vizquel SS (35)
Ellis Burks DH (37)
Jim Thome 1B (31)
Travis Fryman 3B (33)
Ricky Gutierrez 2B (31)
Milton Bradley CF (23)
Russell Branyan LF (26)
Einar Diaz C (29)
Bartolo Colon P (28)

By the time the Indians would indeed contend in 2005, not a single player from this lineup would be with the team. Nor would anyone from the Robbie Alomar deal (although Billy Traber would be in the minors, trying to come back from major elbow surgery).

The Indians were in the midst of a massive public relations crisis. Shapiro was viewed suspiciously by most fans. It was John Hart who built the Tribe of the 1990s, not Shapiro. Yes, he was part of the front office, but Hart was the front man. Hart made the big decisions. For a while, Shapiro was minor league director, then assistant general manager. The fans didn't know what he did. Nor was he like Mike Hargrove, a terrific player for the Tribe in the dark ages of the old Stadium, then the manager who led them into the light during the Jacobs Field era. Hart and Hargrove built the Indians, backed by owner Dick Jacobs. And he was gone, too.

In 2002, all of them were gone. Here were the Dolans, seemingly presiding over a once proud country that suddenly couldn't fix its roads or make buses run on time. And here was Shapiro, younger than most of them at thirty-six, an agent's son with an Ivy League education who had never played, coached, or managed a single inning of professional baseball.

The fans had doubts, and for good reason, since things had been getting worse ever since they assumed ownership.

A fan wrote me this letter after the Colon trade:

> I fear that this trade (and the others to follow) will be the Rocky Colavito deal for my children. I grew up emulating Colavito when I stepped to the plate in Little League. His trade was devastating to me. Now, my kids whose bedrooms have street signs *Jim Thome Avenue* and *Omar Vizquel Drive* on their walls wait for the other shoe to drop . . . They know it's a business. Until now, that hasn't hit home with trades of their favorite players from their favorite teams. My kids have no memory of the Indians being anything other than a contender . . . The Dolans and Shapiro can't be serious . . . if you are going to build a team around pitching, it usually helps to start with an ace.

Another fan wrote:

> This looks like nothing more than a fire sale/house cleaning. Don't be surprised if Dolan keeps cutting payroll then sells the team . . . so much for pitching and defense . . . no one is going to believe anything Dolan or his stooge Shapiro say in the future.

There were many letters like those. Most voiced anger and fear. Anger because it seemed the best players were leaving. Fear that the new ones would not be worthy of a place in the hearts of the fans, especially when the mantra wasn't just "contend in 2005," it was "cut the budget, cut the budget, cut the budget."

Even before the Colon trade, ownership really hurt itself. It was soon after the Robbie Alomar deal with the Mets, and Larry Dolan was speaking to a group in Akron. The 2002 season had yet to begin. The elder Dolan stood up, and the first thing he said was "Who's Robbie Alomar?"

The people groaned.

In 2001, Alomar hit .336 with 20 homers, 100 RBI, and 30 stolen bases and won a Gold Glove. Who's Robbie Alomar? To the fans, he was a star, someone to cheer for, even if he could be moody. Robbie Alomar could play and seemed on his way to the Hall of Fame when the Indians traded him.

Then Larry Dolan launched into a discussion of how fans "should never fall in love with the assets." He meant the players. I sat in that crowd, looking at the fans' faces and thinking, "This guy just doesn't get it."

Most fans at the luncheon were thinking, "Who's Larry Dolan to criticize Robbie Alomar?"

From a business standpoint, he was absolutely correct. Baseball front offices have made far more mistakes by hanging on to players too long than trading stars too early. In fact, one of the commandments for executives is "It's always better to trade a guy one year too soon than one year too late." But at the same time, fans are expected to buy tickets to cheer for a team. This was not like purchasing a mutual fund. Baseball is an emotional experience fueled by winning, and fans become attached to the players. Dolan should have praised Alomar, praised the players coming in the trade, and generally stayed upbeat. I wrote a column about Larry Dolan's "Assets Speech," and it was not something the owner would have kept for his scrapbook. When you were replacing Robbie Alomar with Ricky Gutierrez—which is how it looked to the fans—you have nothing to brag about.

•   •   •

One of the least relevant criticisms made about the Colon trade was that Indians shouldn't be unloading talent while they were still in contention. Let's face it, they were 7½ games behind the Twins and had just lost six of eight games.

"I heard from fans that we gave up on the season too early," Tom Hamilton said. "I asked them if they had watched us play. We were going nowhere. I knew we were not going to be able to sign Colon, and that we needed lots of prospects. I knew Montreal had the best farm system in baseball. I knew nothing about the players we were getting. I knew this trade was going to make or break the franchise, but I felt they had to make it. You looked in our minor league system, basically no one was there."

One person on the Indians staff who wasn't so eager to write off the rest of the season was manager Charlie Manuel, who wanted to keep his job. Regarding the Colon trade, Manuel was "in the loop, but on the periphery," according to Shapiro. Shapiro told Manuel what he was thinking and why he believed the deal had to be made. He would have preferred for Manuel to support the deal, but Shapiro knew better. Pretend you were Charlie Manuel. You were not hired by Shapiro, but by John Hart. You were brought in to get the team back to the World Series. They fired Mike Hargrove after the 1999 season when Hargrove won 97 games before collapsing in the playoffs. Hart mentioned that Manuel was replacing Hargrove to "help get us to the next level." Those words bothered Hargrove back then, and still do.

"I would not have minded if they said the team needed to hear another voice, or something like that," said Hargrove. "But to say the next level . . . "

Hargrove had managed the Indians to the World Series in 1995 and 1997. Was he to blame for the failure to win the ultimate championship? Did he do a lousy job in 1999 when the team won 97 games?

Manuel and Hart had been close ever since managing against

each other in the minors. It was Hart's idea to bring Manuel into the Tribe system as a minor league manager, where he was very successful. It also was Hart who promoted Manuel to the team's hitting coach on Hargrove's staff, a job Manuel also did extremely well. Most people close to the team knew that if Hart ever fired Hargrove, Manuel would be the next manager. There was no question, Manuel was Hart's guy.

Manuel was brought in to lead a veteran team and to win big. It was Shapiro's decision to keep Manuel. Why not? He managed the Indians to 90 and 91 wins in his first two seasons, and a Central Division title in 2001. Manuel was a solid manager, despite his Blue Ridge Mountains accent and bizarre sentence structure. He related to most players. He wasn't a modern manager in terms of using all forms of statistical data, but he knew the game and understood most players. Hargrove was no fan of Manuel's but grudgingly admitted, "Charlie is sly as a fox, don't underestimate him."

But when the Colon trade was made, Manuel was fifty-eight years old. He had been in the hospital several times in the previous two years with various physical problems. He was not the right manager for Shapiro's new plan. The last thing he wanted to hear about was contending in three years, because he knew he'd be long gone by then.

"I don't think Charlie had a real understanding of why the trade had to happen," said Shapiro. "He's a conventional major league manager, and what we were doing was very unconventional. I'm sure there was some concern about what it meant for him."

Not just Manuel, but nearly everyone in the clubhouse wondered if they'd be around by the end of the season. That was especially true for veterans such as Travis Fryman, Omar Vizquel, Paul Shuey, Chuck Finley, Ricardo Rincon, Ellis Burks, and Jim Thome. Shapiro addressed the team after the Colon trade, and it was the first time he'd talked to them as a group in the clubhouse.

He didn't think that was the job of a general manager because the clubhouse should be controlled by the manager—unless there were some exceptional circumstances. The Colon trade certainly fit into that category.

"My job is to have one eye on now and one eye on the future," Shapiro told the players. "Your job is to have both eyes on now. There are times when that vision splits in our separate interests."

Shapiro explained how the farm system had to be rebuilt and why Colon was the best person to trade to make that happen. He made no promises about the future, and, in fact, indicated there probably would be more trades. Several of the players were unhappy, for obvious reasons. Then Fryman stood up and said, "Listen, this guy is a GM of a big league team. He doesn't have to come down here. He doesn't have to explain himself. Yet he has the respect for us to come down here and explain what he did. That's his job, and our job is to play."

Those words ended the meeting. But certainly not the doubts.

Manuel was very worried. His contract was up at the end of the season, and he had no assurances that he'd be given an extension. In fact, trading veterans meant he would be fired, at least in his own mind. The team would lose, and when that happens, the manager takes the fall—especially when the general manager didn't hire the manger in the first place. I had several private discussions with Manuel about this, and he mentioned that during the All-Star break, he planned to have a talk with Shapiro about his future. It sounded like a good idea. I also thought it would not turn out well for Manuel. Shapiro was not about to commit to Manuel or anyone else at this point. But Manuel needed clarity. He needed to confront his boss.

Manuel went to see Shapiro with one question that needed to be answered: "Am I your guy or not?" If so, Manuel wanted a contract extension so everyone would know that he would be around next year.

"It's been characterized, mostly by Charlie, that I had already made up my mind [about him]. And I truly hadn't made up my mind," said Shapiro. "We were in a massive state of flux and change. I had started this thing, and Charlie felt it was unfair to him—and some of it was . . . Guys wanted to know where they stood, and Charlie wanted to know where he stood. He knew there was crap flying around the clubhouse."

Let's assume Shapiro is correct, that he had not come to any final conclusion about Manuel. But let's also look at this through the eyes of Manuel. He had been with the Indians organization for twelve years. He and Shapiro both rose through the ranks. When Shapiro said he needed time to think and to "see how this plays out," Manuel wondered, what was there to think about? In Manuel's mind, there was nothing more he could prove to Shapiro. They already knew each other, and down deep, Manuel sensed he was not Shapiro's ideal manager. Manuel was down-home, old-school baseball. Shapiro was the new breed, blazing a new trail with a bunch of new people around him who had not known Manuel for long. The reason Manuel wanted to know from Shapiro, "Am I your guy?" was that he was sure he was not Shapiro's guy. And by the end of the meeting, Manuel was no longer the manager. You can decide if he was fired or quit . . . or quit before he was fired. But he was out.

Afterwards, both men confided to me that they were "relieved." This was a baseball marriage that could not be saved.

Shapiro promoted coach Joel Skinner to manager, a perfect choice for an interim position. Skinner, a savvy baseball guy who caught in the majors for nine years, worked his way up through the Tribe farm system as a manager before becoming a Tribe coach in 2001. He's a quiet, patient man. His father, Bob Skinner, had been a major league player and manager. Joel Skinner had been around the game his entire life. He was forty-one years old, and this was his first chance to manage in the majors. Unlike Manuel, who sometimes feared the Indians could be his last managerial job if things turned ugly, Skinner knew time was on his side. He liked young players, and wasn't afraid to follow the lead of the front office and play kids—and take losses—if that was the current plan. A man of deep faith with four children, Skinner did not view every game as life and death, or even the job as the essence of who he is as a person. Many people say they value God, family, and work in that order. Few are able to keep those priorities lined up as well as Skinner.

"After the Colon deal, we asked ourselves who else were our marketable guys," said Shapiro. "It was basically gloves off on about every guy."

When Shapiro continued to make trades, Skinner could handle it.

Chuck Finley was traded to St. Louis for first baseman Luis Garcia and a player to be named later. Finley was thirty-nine, and making $9 million on the last year of his contract. There was $4 million left on the deal, and the Indians agreed to pay it. Just like in the Colon deal, they were "buying" prospects.

Garcia was supposed to be the key guy to trade. He was converted from pitcher to a right-handed power hitter. He had hit 20 and 26 homers in his previous two minor league seasons.

Here was the Tribe's consensus scouting report:

> Second division starter or platoon player. Has power and should hit some HRs. Questions about the bat, stroke has some length and he tends to pull off the ball . . . He will need to be more disciplined and selective at plate . . . Defensively, has good actions at 1B and moves around the bag well . . . Somewhat low key personality.

Garcia never made it with the Indians, and reading this report, you can understand why.

But the "player to be named later" did.

When the Indians announced Coco Crisp as the other part of the deal, it rated four sentences in the *Akron Beacon Journal*. He was a footnote just about everywhere else.

"We had three teams after Finley, and we talked about twenty prospects with those three teams," said Shapiro. "We rated them 1 to 20. Then we rated them 1 to 12. We had gotten Garcia, and he was in our top twelve. But when it came to the other guys, we ended up taking Coco. He was number thirteen on our list. We had three scouts watch him, and all three believed he'd eventually make the majors as a fourth outfielder. No one thought he'd hit for the kind of power that he has shown."

Shapiro was thinking quality and quantity when it came to these deals. He wanted at least two prospects for Finley. While scouts preferred Garcia, Shapiro's people who looked at statistics were intrigued by Crisp. At twenty-one, he was selected the St. Louis Cardinals' Minor League Player of the Year when he batted .306 with 11 homers and 47 RBI at Class A Potomac in 2001.

When he was acquired in 2002, Crisp was in Class AA batting .301 with nine homers and 47 RBI in 89 games. At twenty-two, Crisp was one of the youngest players in the Eastern League. Crisp didn't throw well. He didn't walk a lot. But he also didn't strike out much, had above-average speed—and everywhere he played, he hit for a high average.

The Tribe's consensus scouting report read:

> Projects as average everyday player . . . Should be able to stay in CF. Swing is similar from both sides of the plate . . . Starts with a wide stance, good short path with good bat speed . . . Has the ability to handle the better off speed pitches . . . Has the ability to drive the ball in the gap and has surprising power. He should hit a few HRs in the big leagues. Aggressive baserunner, plays hard.

Crisp finished the 2002 season with the Indians batting .260 in 127 at-bats. He virtually skipped over Class AAA (playing only four games that year) before joining the Tribe. Finley never pitched after 2002. Crisp became the Tribe's starting outfielder in 2004. Garcia has played in the minors with other teams.

Shapiro dealt Paul Shuey to the Dodgers for Ricardo Rodriguez, who was rated the Dodgers' Top Prospect by *Baseball America*. I loved his arm, but Rodriguez had several injuries and was traded to Texas for Ryan Ludwick, who has kept getting hurt. The Indians also obtained Francisco Cruceta in that deal. He also failed to stick with the Tribe.

The Tribe's consensus scouting report on Rodriguez read:

> No. 2 starter in the future. His fastball topped out at 94 mph. Best pitch is his slider, needs a better changeup . . . Maximum effort delivery spinning out on front leg, getting sideways. Needs better rhythm and balance. Very good looking prospect with average control.

Apparently, I wasn't the only one who liked Rodriguez. It's possible that his wild delivery led to his arm problems. But this was a deal that should have worked out better, at least on paper. But so many don't, regardless of the scouting. Injuries are dream breakers for scouts as well as players.

Ricky Rincon was traded to Oakland for a minor league infielder who didn't make it. The Indians did get out of the remaining $1 million on his contract.

A significant deal in 2002 shipped Russell Branyan to the Reds for Ben Broussard, who became a useful first baseman for the Tribe. While the Indians have looked for an upgrade at first base, Broussard has held the position since 2004.

The Tribe's consensus scouting report on Broussard:

> Big burly body guy with bat value . . . Defensive skills limited to playing first base . . . Struggled vs. LHP, bailed out and took defensive swings. Much better vs. RHP. Drove the ball to all fields with HR power. Short stroke, hard contact. Plays hard, works at game.

It's notable that Broussard, Sizemore, and Crisp all were praised for their work ethic and attitude by the scouts, and all of them exceeded the basic scouting reports. The Indians became obsessed with collecting prospects, counting on their scouting and development people to turn these guys into major leaguers.

"We still spent a lot of money, despite the trades," said Paul Dolan. "We paid the salaries of Colon, Finley, and Shuey for that season. Our payroll for that year ended up at about $82 million, which is what we projected. We lost more than $10 million. The trades were really not about cutting payroll, they were about getting prospects."

Beginning with the Robbie Alomar deal, followed by all the others in 2002, the Indians obtained twenty-two prospects of varying caliber. But suddenly, they had numbers on their side, and by the end of the season, their farm system was ranked number one in baseball by *USA Today Baseball Weekly.*

At the end of the season, Shapiro made what appeared to be just a so-so deal when he sent Ryan Drese and Einar Diaz to John Hart in Texas for Travis Hafner. Some scouts liked Hafner, some didn't. The primary concern was his lack of position. But Hafner has turned out to be a premier designated hitter, and that deal would rank right below the Colon trade in terms of putting the Indians back into contention.

The Tribe's consensus scouting report on Hafner:

Potential middle of the order LH bat. Has power potential with a solid idea of how to hit . . . Disciplined, has good knowledge of strike zone . . . hangs in well vs. LHP. Average bat speed with above average strength . . . Uses the whole field to hit with slight upper cut . . . Aggressive, yet selective . . . Very limited defensively at 1B . . . Mountain of a man. Has had some injuries, needs to stay healthy . . . Tough guy who works at his game.

Another player praised for his attitude and dedication. And his plate discipline. Notice how the reports on Hafner, Sizemore, and Crisp differed from Escobar's. All three hitters made consistent contact and were disciplined. They lacked Escobar's innate athletic skills, but they were simply better baseball players in terms of swinging the bat.

Of those twenty-two prospects, the ones who have made an impact with the Tribe are Lee, Sizemore, Crisp, Hafner, and Broussard. That's 5 of 22, about 18 percent, which is better than the usual 8 to 12 rate when it comes to developing players and them having somewhat significant careers.

With all the attention paid to the prospects in 2002, it's almost possible to overlook the fact that the Tribe's most popular veteran, Jim Thome, batted .304 with 52 homers and 118 RBI. He also became a free agent.

CHAPTER 8

"IF THE INDIANS CAN'T KEEP THIS GUY, THEY WON'T KEEP ANYONE."

JIM THOME LEAVES

Jim Thome leaving may have begun with Matt Lawton coming.

Make that the Matt Lawton contract, the four-year, $27 million extension the outfielder received when he came to the Indians in the trade for Robbie Alomar. Lawton officially joined the Indians on December 11, 2001, and his extension was announced six days later.

That contract would haunt the Indians in so many ways.

When he was acquired by the Indians, Lawton was one year away from free agency, which made him eligible for arbitration. Arbitration is a process in which the player's agent and the team submit numbers and an independent arbitrator picks which salary seems to be the most fair. Lawton was making $3.5 million at the time. In arbitration, he very well could have been awarded $6 million. In 2001 he hit a combined .277 with 36 doubles, 13 homers, 64 RBI, and 29 steals for the Mets and Twins. He was a career .275 hitter, thirty years old, in the prime of his career.

"The paradigm then was to lock up the players you liked before free agency, if possible," said Shapiro. "A year after this trade, everything changed."

Lawton had never had a long-term contract and was anxious to get some security. Yes, a player like Lawton talks about needing "security." He had just made $3.5 million that year. He had been paid more than $6 million in his pro career by the age of twenty-nine. If you can't figure out a way to be secure on that much cash, you never will. This is not to pick on Lawton; it's just to inject a little reality. Thome would later fall into the same trap, debating the Indians' failure to guarantee a sixth year on his offer. It's not really about security, it's about making money, and often about comparing the money you make to what another player is paid. Yes, they say money can't buy you love. But in pro sports, it can make you *feel* loved.

At least for a little while.

Lawton was all warm and fuzzy after signing that extension. New Tribe second baseman Ricky Gutierrez also was thrilled after signing a three-year, $11 million deal with the Tribe as a free agent. Thome, however, was confused and upset, wondering why he hadn't received what he thought was a fair offer to extend his contract after all he'd done for the Indians—especially after seeing what these new guys—not even All-Stars—were getting paid.

"I know Jimmy was disappointed that Lawton and Gutierrez were taken care of first," said broadcaster Tom Hamilton, who was close to Thome. "Jim and I had talked, and he was hurt by that. I know you have to separate business and personal feelings, but I also felt, 'Some guys will just shrug it off, but this is a guy, if he's hurt, it will mean more.' Jimmy is a very principled guy, a very loyal guy. I was very worried about what may happen with Jimmy by the end of the season."

Thome also mentioned it to a few teammates and some friends in the lower level of the front office. Certainly Thome was not about to sign for Lawton's money. He was already making $8 million for 2002. In 2001, he batted .291 with 49 homers and 124 RBI, the best season of his career. He was the Tribe's all-time home run leader. He was putting together what appeared to be a Hall of Fame career. A native of Peoria, Illinois, Thome liked Cleveland and wanted to stay in the Midwest.

Shapiro had been talking with Thome's agent. The Indians made an offer, which was rejected. The only time Thome ever got angry about something I wrote was in the spring of 2002, when I included a brief note in my Sunday column saying that his agent turned down a four-year, $42 million extension. Three members of the Tribe front office told me how upset Thome was about the item. I wasn't surprised Thome's agent rejected the offer: it seemed low to me. Thome tried to tell me that no real offer had been made, and that by writing what I did, I made him look bad. This is where a player and writer can play the semantics game. Perhaps the Indians didn't make any offer in writing, so technically no offer was made. Other times, an agent doesn't tell the player about an offer made by the team—he simply rejects it. I'm not saying this was the case with Thome. But I am positive about the four-year offer made in the spring of 2002. A high-ranking member of the Tribe front office confirmed it when I learned of it—and before I wrote it. When interviewed for this book, Shapiro said, "We did offer Jim an extension in spring training, and it was turned down." His agent also informed the Indians there would be no more talks until after the season, as they planned to explore free agency.

I believe Thome hated all the talk about money in baseball. Yes, he was going to be a free agent. The decision had been made that he'd play out the final year of his contract and see what the market would pay. But he didn't want to talk about money, nor did he want anyone writing about money and his pending free agency. Most sports writers don't enjoy dealing with that kind of story, either. But this story was going to make a major impact on the Indians, and Thome was perhaps their most popular player. The only other Tribe player who came close was Omar Vizquel.

So Thome was struggling with the decision, even before the first pitch of the regular season. It's hard to know what his agent or others were telling him, but it's clear Thome had seen Albert

Belle, Manny Ramirez, and Kenny Lofton all leave as free agents. The last player to come through the Tribe system and be re-signed to a long-term deal was Charles Nagy, who signed a four-year, $17 million extension that would expire at the end of 2002. The Indians did offer Ramirez a huge contract, and it seemed they'd make a big bid for Thome. But there also seemed to be this momentum of players leaving as free agents. Some were upset with long-term contracts they signed early in their careers that came to seem like bargains for the team when they developed into stars. Thome was not one of those, but Ramirez supposedly was bothered by that. Or at least, someone told Ramirez that he had to realize the Indians somehow took advantage of him when he signed his first extension. In Manny's situation, it was hard to know what he thought because it changed as frequently as he changed agents.

Thome seemed a bit shaken by all the turnover in 2002. John Hart left as general manager, and that may have had some impact—but not a lot. The firing of Charlie Manuel really hurt. Thome had known Manuel since 1992 when they were together at Class AAA Colorado Springs. Consider that in 1992, Thome played at Class AA Akron and Class AAA Buffalo and played 40 games in the majors with the Tribe. In 272 at-bats that season, he had a mere five homers. The previous year, he had hit eight. There was no sign of what Thome would become until 1993. But Manuel had believed in him.

"He'd been up with Cleveland and everyone felt like they'd given him a chance and he failed," Manuel told reporters in 2001. "They said he couldn't hit, and he couldn't play third base. I said, 'I'm the AAA manager, I'll take him to Charlotte with me, and when Jimmy is twenty-five or twenty-six he's going to hit 40 homers and bat .320 with 100 RBI, you can mark it down.'"

Thome opened the 1993 season at Class AAA Charlotte, where Manuel was managing. The two men had developed a friendship in the previous season, when they were together for two months. Manuel had projected Thome as a home run hitter, but hadn't wanted to make major changes to the kid's left-handed swing in the middle of the season. But in 1993, Manuel began to show Thome how to pull the ball, how to get more of his legs and hips into his swing—creating fly balls that seemed to carry and carry and carry. In 1993, Thome hammered 25 homers in 115 games in the International League, and he hit seven more with the Tribe in 47 games. That gave him 32 homers. In his previous four pro seasons, he'd had only 29 homers.

Manuel changed the direction of Thome's career, and the player never forgot that. In 1994, Thome opened the season at third base for the Indians, and Manuel was there as the team's new hitting coach. The two men were constantly in the batting cage, working on Thome's swing. They often talked hitting. Manuel, by nature a positive teacher, knew how to make Thome believe in himself. In that Blue Ridge Mountain accent, Manuel sometimes called him, "Tome Dome," and the two men with rural backgrounds instantly connected. Thome continued to hit for power, and Manuel was there for every game. When Thome hit his 242nd career homer to tie Albert Belle for the Indians' team record, he gave the ball to Manuel. When Manuel was promoted to manager, Thome was thrilled. Not because he had any problems with Mike Hargrove, but simply because no one had had a bigger impact on his career than Manuel. But when Thome saw the Robbie Alomar trade, the Bartolo Colon trade, and all the other changes, he not only knew the end of the Tribe as a contender was near, he knew that his friend Charlie Manuel was not going to be managing the team for long.

Manuel was gone from the manager's office at the All-Star break, fired on July 11, 2002.

Another blow came when Indians trainer Jimmy Warfield died suddenly five days later.

"Within a week, Jimmy lost two of the people on the team who were the closest to him," said Tribe public relations director Bart Swain. "He didn't just lose a manager in Charlie, but he lost his mentor. And Jimmy Warfield had been there from Day One that Jimmy arrived in Cleveland. Now he was gone. He continued to play well, but both of those things sent him reeling."

Thome never said this. He continued to insist he enjoyed playing in Cleveland. He politely brushed off questions about his free agency. On the field, he was the ultimate pro. In 2002, he set a franchise record with 52 homers, batting .304 with 118 RBI while often unprotected in a Tribe lineup that had suddenly turned anemic through trades, injuries, and age. There were a dozen different players used in the number five spot behind Thome. Like the fans, Thome had become used to the Indians being a powerhouse in the Central Division. Now he saw veteran talent leaving, the budget being cut. He heard the team's general manager talking about not contending again until 2005. He was thirty-two at the end of the 2002 season. To a player at that stage of his career, three years waiting to contend again sounded like thirty, especially since there were no guarantees it would happen.

The Indians made no attempt to trade Thome during the 2002 season because they thought they had a chance to re-sign him. Thome also had a no-trade clause, his wife was pregnant with their first child, and he told the Indians he didn't want to move her during the season.

"Intellectually, the right thing was not to sign Jimmy to the kind of contract being discussed at the end of the season," said Shapiro. "His salary would have hog-tied our organization. But he stood for everything we wanted to stand for. He epitomized what we're about as an organization."

Immediately after the season, the Indians heard there would be two serious bidders for Thome—Baltimore and Philadelphia. But the Orioles never made an impressive offer. Philadelphia was a different story, one the Tribe knew well. The Phillies were moving into a new ballpark and wanted to sign some free agents to sell tickets and stir interest. And the new park with its suites and luxury boxes would create income to help pay for the new players.

"We really did try to keep Thome," said Paul Dolan. "Our original four-year [$42 million] offer was probably the right one for a player his age. But Jimmy was special to us and to the fans. He's like Bob Feller, you wanted him to finish his career here and be a part of the community. People respond to him."

The Indians put together a five-year deal worth $60 million. There was a sixth year with only $2 million of the $14 million guaranteed. Add it all up, and Thome would received $62 million, guaranteed. The Indians tried to be creative. They also offered the following:

- A no-trade clause
- A luxury suite at every game for his family, friends, or anyone else
- A Jim Thome video from which he'd be paid the profits
- Two amateur baseball fields built each year in his name
- A section of Jacobs Field named the Jim Thome Home Run Porch; every time he hit a home run to that section, a donation to charity would be made in his name
- A statue of Thome outside Jacobs Field, like the one of Bob Feller
- A personal services contract worth $250,000 annually for ten years after he retired
- A $500,000 bonus if he was voted to the Hall of Fame, and a street near Jacobs Field named after him.

The Indians laid out these perks in an elaborate presentation, explaining how players such as Brooks Robinson (Baltimore),

Kirby Puckett (Minnesota), and Carl Yastrzemski (Boston) ben-efited from spending their entire careers with one team.

Philadelphia responded by piling on the money and the years: six years, $87 million.

That meant Thome would be thirty-eight in the final season.

"In an offer that long, Jimmy's age and health became an issue," said Paul Dolan. "There was no way we could match that."

The Indians also tried to sell Thome on the advantage of stay-ing in the American League. He knew the pitchers. He always hit well in Jacobs Field—it was a comfort zone. He could be the designated hitter as he got older, while in the National League, he would always have to play first base. He'd had some back and other problems; the option of being a DH could extend his career and help his chances for the Hall of Fame.

"People said we made this offer because we knew Thome wouldn't take it and we wanted to offer just enough to look good," said Paul Dolan. "That's giving us too much credit for knowing where that sweet spot is. The offer was made in good faith. If Manny or Thome had taken those offers, we planned to honor them. We were sincere."

Sincere, but probably too late.

Had the Indians made this offer at the end of the 2001 season—and before Lawton received his extension—odds are Thome would have accepted it. He may have even told them to skip all the extras about statues and home run porches, just give money to charity. Thome was active in so many civic projects. But the Indians waited too long to become daring and creative. Thome might have sensed the organization was hesitant to commit to anyone for the long haul, and he was right. The baseball labor agreement was pending, attendance was dropping, a rebuilding effort was coming. How did Thome fit into that?

There may have been other factors. For example, the Players Association often puts subtle pressure on a free agent to grab the biggest offer, because that can help raise salaries for other free agents—or at least that's their argument. Thome strongly denied that the union, his agent, his wife, or anyone else made an impact on his decision. But this is a bottom-line business where the bottom line is just that—the bottom line.

Thome took the money in Philadelphia. He was emotional and not focused at the press conference announcing his signing. Twice he said he wanted to retire with the Indians. It was a strange comment on a day when he was signing with another team. He said he would have stayed in Cleveland had the Indians offered him a sixth year guaranteed. Then he also said he didn't sign in Cleveland because "I didn't want to saddle them with my contract in five years."

Listening to that press conference, I sensed Thome still wasn't sure what he wanted to do. He was conflicted, moving to an East Coast city that really didn't fit his lifestyle. But he was gone.

"I knew the backlash would be severe," said Paul Dolan. "Of all the players we lost, the worst was Thome."

Bart Swain remembered the onslaught of calls—"How can you let this guy go? He's a legend! I'm canceling my season tickets."

Some fans said the Dolans were cheap, some compared the owners and Shapiro to Art Modell, the owner/traitor who moved the Browns to Baltimore. Fans saw Alomar, Colon, and Thome leave in a twelve-month period. Ramirez had gone before that. With the exception of Omar Vizquel, every player they had come to really know from the glory days of the late 1990s was now gone. It was happening under the watch of the Dolans, and it didn't matter to the fans that the owners had spent the two biggest payrolls in team history.

To the fans, the Indians seemed hopeless.

"If the Indians can't keep this guy, they won't keep anyone," fans told Tom Hamilton.

•　　•　　•

During the Thome talks, Shapiro was working on another deal—this one with old friend John Hart of the Rangers. Shapiro and Hart would talk often. ("I've never made a major baseball decision without consulting John," said Shapiro.) Shapiro knew that Thome was probably gone, but even if Thome did stay, he wanted another hitter, a Thome-type guy. His scouts, especially Gary Tuck, believed they had found one in Travis Hafner, a Class AAA first baseman/DH for the Rangers. Hafner is a Moneyball kind of player, the type favored by the statistical system whose strongest advocate is Oakland GM Bill Beane. It's based on a statistic called OPS—On base Plus Slugging. You add a player's on-base percentage to his slugging percentage and you come up with a number. On base not only reflects the player's frequency of getting on base, but shows if the player is a disciplined hitter. Does he draw walks? Remember in Little League where some coaches would say, "A walk is as good as a hit"? Well, the on-base percentage mirrors that thinking.

When Hafner played at Class AAA Oklahoma City in 2002, he led the Pacific Coast League with a .463 on-base percentage, a stunning number. Anything over .400 is excellent; over .350 is very good.

Hafner's slugging percentage was .559.

The magic number for OPS is 1.000, and few players at any level achieve it.

In 2002, Hafner's OPS was 1.012! His more traditional statistics also glittered: .342 with 21 homers and 77 RBI in 110 games. Word was that Hafner's defense was awful. But with offense like that . . .

He was twenty-five, and had had a brief trial with the Rangers in 2002, hitting only .242 with one homer and six RBI in 62 at-bats.

This was a perfect match.

Hart was on the prowl for pitching (as he had always been for the Indians). He liked Ryan Drese, who had just had one very strange season for the Tribe. In 2002, Drese's record was 10–9 for a team that finished 74–88. But his earned run average was an outrageously high 6.55. He was shelled for 176 hits in 137 innings. You don't want a pitcher to allow more hits than innings pitched. His 102 strikeouts in 137 innings were respectable—you like a pitcher to average about seven strikeouts per nine innings. Drese had above-average ability, a 93 mph fastball, and a couple of decent breaking pitches. After a sad performance, he'd tell the media how some of the balls weren't hit that hard and how the umpire missed a call, basically saying none of it was his fault. He did not seem very receptive to coaching at this stage of his career.

Meanwhile, Shapiro's reports were that Hafner had a tremendous attitude and was a real team player with a desire to improve. He was from Sykeston, North Dakota, where his high school graduating class numbered eight: "Four girls and four boys, so everyone could have a prom date," Hafner once said. He was a 31st-round pick by Texas, and slowly worked his way through the Ranger farm system before his breakout season in 2002. A buffalo of a man, he has wide shoulders, strong legs, a six-foot-four, 255-pound build with low body fat. As Shapiro said, "Physically, he's a monster." And he was a disciplined left-handed hitter.

The negatives were some past surgery on his right wrist and elbow . . . and his defense. The guy seemed to wrestle most balls to the ground like a member of the Secret Service, rather than fielding them.

The scouts tried not to press the comparisons hard, but there were some obvious similarities to Thome—in size, style of hitting, and personality.

"We were making the trade regardless of what happened with Thome," said Shapiro. "If we kept Jim, then Travis could DH. He was a special hitter and we wanted him very much."

Shapiro was aware that Hart longed for Drese. He also knew the Tribe payroll was being cut from $82 million in 2002 to under $50 million in 2003. He was looking for ways to dump contracts. Catcher Einar Diaz was set to make $1.8 million in 2003, and $2.9 million in 2004. He was coming off a dismal season where he hit only .206 with two homers in 102 games in 2002. Shapiro had Victor Martinez coming, the switch-hitting catcher who'd won the Class AA Eastern League batting title (.336, 22 HR, 85 RBI), and also Josh Bard, another switch-hitting catcher, who hit .297 at Class AAA Buffalo. He believed Bard could start for a year or two until Martinez was ready. There was no reason to keep Diaz.

Hart liked Diaz, a good-natured player who had batted .281, .272, and .277 in the three years before 2002. Diaz had little power, rarely walked, but was considered an average defensive catcher—and respectable catchers are always of value. So the trade became Drese and Diaz for Hafner and minor league pitcher Aaron Myette. The Rangers had written off Hafner because they had veteran Rafael Palmeiro at first base.

It's often revealing to look back at what was said on the day of the deal, and here are Shapiro's initial comments on Hafner: "This is not a stop-gap guy. We have been tracking him since the start of spring training [2002]. He's one of the most unique hitters in the minors. He hits for average and power, and he gets on base and he walks. We were going to trade for him no matter what happened with Thome."

Shapiro also hyped Myette, talking about his 97 mph fastball and comparing the right-hander to Steve Karsay, whom the Indians had picked up a few years earlier and turned into one of the more successful setup relievers in the majors before sending him to Atlanta in the dreadful John Rocker deal.

Myette never did anything for the Tribe. Hafner has become a star. At the time of the deal, I remember writing that maybe Hart had done the Tribe a favor. He was the guy who traded Richie Sexson, Sean Casey, and Brian Giles for pitching. This deal smelled of that kind of desperation again, only this time it could be perfume to the Tribe.

Fans know what happened to Thome and Hafner.

In his first two years, Thome was sensational in Philadelphia, averaging 45 homers and 120 RBI. Hafner started slowly in 2003, and needed a trip back to the minors for a refresher course. But in the next two years, he averaged 31 homers and 108 RBI, hitting .308. In 2005, his OPS was 1.003, the second highest in the American League, right behind Alex Rodriguez. In each of those seasons, he had exactly a .410 on-base percentage.

In 2005, Thome turned thirty-four. He went on the disabled list twice. He had back and elbow problems. He lost his first-base job to rookie Ryan Howard. He hit .207 with seven homers and 30 RBI. He was traded to the White Sox for Aaron Rowland and two top pitching prospects, the Phillies paying $22 million of the $46 million left on the three years of his contract.

"If Jim had taken our contract offer, we'd have been in trouble," said Shapiro. "We would not have been able to sign Kevin Millwood or Bob Wickman for 2005. Our payroll would not have been going up enough to come close to handling his contract and allowing us to make other moves."

Hafner has replaced Thome. And he signed a contract extension keeping him with the team through 2007. Thome entered the spring of 2006 at thirty-five, needing to prove he's healthy.

CHAPTER 9

"I NEVER FELT TOO YOUNG TO MANAGE."

ERIC WEDGE TAKES CHARGE

When the 2002 season ended, most fans believed Joel Skinner would remain as the Tribe manager, and so did the team's owners.

"I went to Mark [Shapiro] and asked why we needed to even go through the process of interviewing for a new manager," said Paul Dolan. "I thought we had our guy in Joel. He did well in the second half of the season. The players liked him and didn't quit on him after we made all the trades. The organization liked him. I liked him. No one had any negatives about Joel."

Shapiro agreed that Skinner did a good job, and said he had tremendous respect for the man who replaced Charlie Manuel at the All-Star break.

"But I want you to talk to Eric Wedge," Shapiro told Dolan.

I remember several conversations with Shapiro after the season. I thought Skinner was solid, but agreed with Shapiro that he should consider others. I knew nothing about Eric Wedge. I did know Shapiro's first choice, Bud Black, and liked him very much. But Black was the pitching coach with the Angels and didn't want to take his family out of Southern California.

"I think every candidate sensed that Bud Black was the front-runner," said Paul Dolan. "But when Bud dropped out, I figured we'd just stay with Joel. There was some talk of getting an experienced major league manager, but the names mentioned were mostly retreads. Lou Piniella wasn't available, but it would have been very hard for a manager like Lou to take this job, because we were rebuilding and developing young players. Most veteran managers want to win right away, and we weren't going to do that. Look how Piniella struggled in Tampa. He's a great manager, but that was hard for him to handle."

Dolan raised a good point. Many veteran managers say they like to develop young players, but they often lack patience. They hate the idea of enduring a few lousy seasons, partly because they don't think they'll survive. Several managers (and head coaches in other sports) have told me, "Here's how it works. The front office says, 'Just play the kids; we'll give you time to develop the players. Don't worry that much about your record, just build a good team for the future.' So you take the hit, play the kids, and lose games. In two years, they fire you because you didn't win enough games. Then another guy comes in, takes the team you developed, and he wins."

It comes down to an issue of trust.

After a manager has been fired a few times, he has trouble having faith in the front office. He often believes the only way he can be sure to keep his job is to win right away, so he plays the guys who give him the best chance of immediate success—while talking about wanting to nurture the prospects. They talk one game and play another, which also angers the front office. The general manager then feels betrayed by the manager, who has abandoned the front office game plan. But in many cases, the manager has reason to be uneasy with the front office. So often the front office does say, be patient with the young players and we'll be patient with you as the manager—and then they fire the manager anyway. Some veteran head coaches and managers become just like players, looking out for number one first and always. One executive described a veteran NBA coach to me as "a 401(k) coach." He meant the coach would do a competent job, but he was in it to protect his position, get another long-term contract, and keep stashing the cash in the 401(k) for retirement, knowing he'd eventually be fired.

Shapiro wanted to avoid this mentality, and that may be part of the reason he avoided hiring a manager simply because he had managed in the majors before. He didn't see this survivor mentality in Skinner, a man of real patience who was dedicated to the Indians.

"Joel's life perspective, his perspective on faith and family and the way he dealt with people were all strengths," said Shapiro. "His confidence and the sense of ease you get in being around him would have enabled him to handle the job. It would not have been a mistake to give it to Joel."

But Shapiro was going to hire his manager in the same way he had been making trades. Not an Alomar deal, with a mixed agenda. A Colon deal. He was out to find the best managerial prospect, period. He didn't care about age. He wasn't set on experience. He was looking for what he called "a difference maker."

He believed that was Eric Wedge, who had been named the 2002 Minor League Manager of the Year by the *Sporting News*.

"But not right away," said Shapiro. "I had him interview with me after the season because I was thinking about him as a member of the coaching staff. The next time around, he could be a candidate for manager."

That makes sense, a very practical approach.

Every GM knows there will come a time that he'll need another manager, even if he loves his current manager. The team could begin to lose. The manager may want to leave. Wedge had never spent a day as a big league coach or manager. He likes to say that isn't important because he was in the majors as a player. But that experience was limited to 86 at-bats in 39 games over small slices of four seasons. Wedge still had a lot to learn about big league baseball. But the more Shapiro talked to Wedge, the more he sensed Wedge was the right guy to handle what was coming—which would be losing while developing young players who would make agonizing mistakes. There would be unfair, often stinging criticism. Wedge was not jaded by broken promises on the big league level. He was anxious to prove himself. He was thirty-four, but looked forty-five and sounded fifty. Not in a world-weary way, but in one that communicated a sense of maturity. Yet with a young man's fire and determination to make a name on baseball's biggest stage, along with the touch of arrogance needed to think he could make it happen.

"I didn't even realize Mark was talking about the manager's job until about halfway through our first interview after the [2002] season," said Wedge. "We had a good year at Buffalo, but I never thought about being a big league manager the next year. I've seen too many people looking too far ahead. I always tell the players to focus on where you are right now. If you look beyond yourself, then you can't get yourself fully into what you want to do."

This is vintage Wedge. Focus on the now; leave tomorrow to tomorrow. Everything is part of a "process," which also is one of Shapiro's favorite words.

Here's part of what Shapiro likes about Wedge: The manager is a true believer. He believes in "respecting the game, respecting your teammates." He believes in treating people fairly. He believes in the needs of the organization and the team, in putting their interests even ahead of his own—such as playing the kids at the minor league level to help them grow, and he'd do it in the big leagues. He believes in the plan that began with the Colon trade.

"Even after that first interview, I wasn't sure where I stood," said Wedge. "I thought Mark had talked to me about the Cleveland job mostly out of respect for the work I did in the minors."

Here is something else that Shapiro appreciated: Wedge played no politics to get the job. He didn't have his friends in baseball call Shapiro to put in a good word. He never said a bad word about Skinner or anyone else who could possibly be considered for the job. He took the same road that he insists his players travel: Take care of your own business, and things will take care of themselves.

Wedge's playing career was mostly one of broken dreams, shattered bones, and endless surgeries. He was a star catcher at Wichita State, a third-round pick by Boston in the 1989 draft. He was supposed to be on the fast track to the majors, a gritty, savvy, and capable catcher with some power. But his knees went. His elbow ached. He just could not stay healthy.

"First it was one knee, then the other," he said. "I had four operations, two on each knee."

There was more.

"My elbow," he said. "Four more surgeries."

In 1992, he batted .299 with 11 homers in 65 games for Class AAA Pawtucket. He was called up to Boston, hit .250 with five homers in 68 at-bats. He was picked in the second round by Colorado in the expansion draft, and seemed destined to get his big league career really started.

But he couldn't throw.

The elbow.

More surgery.

Wedge would play in the minors until 1997, moving from prospect to suspect. He evolved into a veteran like the Crash Davis character in the movie *Bull Durham*. He was there to help the young pitchers, to back the manager, and to prepare himself for baseball life after playing. Wedge first heard from Shapiro before the 1997 season. He was a minor league free agent. Shapiro was the Tribe's farm director, and he wanted a veteran catcher for Buffalo. While the two men liked each other, Wedge ended up signing with the Phillies' Class AAA Scranton/Wilkes-Barre franchise.

"In the middle of that season, my knees were so bad, I could barely walk up a few stairs," he said. "I knew it was over. My knees were shot. My condition was chronic."

Wedge is a stubborn man who hates to admit pain or weakness. He's the son of a Fort Wayne truck driver, growing up where excuses were not accepted. You lived by working hard, gritting your teeth, and staying the course.

"If my father got in my face and yelled, I took it," he said. "He set expectations, and they were clear expectations. If you didn't meet them, there were consequences. My mom was a nurse. We were hard-working people."

With two brittle knees and an aching right elbow, Wedge still was able to play 47 games, hitting seven homers in 129 at-bats with a .256 average at Class AAA. He was not far away from being a big league backup catcher.

Only he limped rather than walked.

"I wanted to keep playing," he said. "I was only 29. Anyone who tells you that they'd rather manage than play is lying. There is nothing like playing. I did what I had to in order to play. Surgeries, shots, rehab . . . all that. When I decided to quit, it was mostly a relief. I was dealing with a lot of pain. A few years into my playing career, I began to think about managing, especially because of my injury situation. I didn't know how long I could play."

Wedge is not a man who opens his emotions to most people. You may find out what he's *thinking*, but seldom will he reveal what he's *feeling*. His career had to be nine years of frustration. Had he been relatively healthy, he had the defensive skills to catch in the big leagues—and backup catchers can last ten, fifteen, or even more years in the majors. Wedge could have been one of those guys, but his body wouldn't allow it. No matter how hard he worked, how much pain he endured, his body betrayed him. His approach was not to weep or grow bitter, but to accept reality. No feeling sorry for yourself in the Wedge household, so he refused to do it. But there had to be some nights when he just wished for one pain-free summer to find out what kind of player he could have become. Knowing Wedge, he refused to allow himself to dwell on that for long.

Bottom line for this bottom-line guy was this: He couldn't play anymore.

When Shapiro and Wedge talked before the 1997 season, Wedge had mentioned an interest in managing or coaching in the minors. After the season, Shapiro heard Wedge had retired as a player, then offered him a chance to manage the Indians' Class A Columbus team. That was a surprise, because Wedge had just turned thirty. Usually, a recently retired player spends a year as a minor league coach before getting the opportunity to manage. The idea is to create a transition in perspective from the small snapshot of the game seen by a player to the big picture of a manager.

"Philadelphia also wanted me to work in their farm system," said Wedge. "I felt I was ready to manage. Catching is a leadership position. I was always comfortable talking to other players, helping them. As I got older, some young players would come and talk to me. I got a lot of satisfaction from that."

That's why Shapiro not only offered Wedge a chance to manage, but skipped over the rookie level and sent him to full-season Class A Columbus, Georgia. Usually, that job went to someone who had spent at least a few years as a minor league manager and coach, but Shapiro believed Wedge was ready, and he kept moving Wedge up the minor league ladder, not just because he was a winning minor league manager, but because Shapiro was convinced that Wedge had the right stuff. He was a natural leader. He understood how to work with the front office, yet he was at home in the dugout and the clubhouse.

"I never felt too young to manage," said Wedge. "I've been doing it for a while, but I still know there's a lot to learn. From the day I quit playing, I promised never to forget three things."

Wedge then pointed to a finger as he mentioned each one: "[One], it's not about me and my career anymore, it's strictly the team. [Two], it's all about making the players better. [Three], never forget how hard it is to play the game.

"For some guys, the longer they are away from their careers, the better players they were and the easier it was to play the game," he said. "I didn't want to be like that. This is a hard, hard game. But when I was talking to Mark about what he planned to do, I wanted the job. I had a belief in his plan. I also had a lot of belief in myself."

Wedge started at Columbus, Georgia, in 1998. By the end of the 2002 season, he was knocking on the door of the manager's office at Jacobs Field.

After their first meeting, Shapiro brought Wedge back for another talk.

"That's when I realized Mark was very serious," said Wedge. "It was going to be either Joel or me getting the job. I wanted to manage in the majors. I had been there as a player. You are competitive and human. You've been there once, you want to get back. But no one could control the timetable."

No one but Shapiro.

"Most guys won't bring a Class AAA manager directly to the majors, because they [general managers] are scared," said Shapiro. "Eric Wedge was thirty-four years old. He had not coached in the big leagues. He had played a total of one-and-a-half big league seasons. Immediately, if he fails, you can find multiple reasons why it didn't work. I talked to [Minor League Director] John Farrell at length. I talked to others who are close to me. I talked to John Hart, to Karl Kuehl, to some other guys who have been around baseball for a long time. But in the end, it comes down to you. You have to pick the guy that you believe in, and you have to live with the consequences."

Shapiro has read a lot of books about leadership. He believes in a system of compiling information, of having a process of evaluation. He rarely goes with his gut. Nor is he especially influenced by public reaction. He knew that to Tribe fans and the media, hiring Wedge would be, at best, a yawner. It wouldn't sell a single ticket or cause even one ripple of anticipation for the coming season. Wedge would be seen as just another faceless, nameless guy in the dugout.

"But down deep, I knew he was the right guy," said Shapiro. "I was looking for a way to speed up the time frame [to get back to contention], and I thought Eric could do that. This is not to diminish Joel Skinner; it's just that I felt so strongly about Eric. I felt Eric's will to win, his burning passion to be the best manager on the planet, and that we shared the same values would make a difference. The most important thing on the face of the earth to him was to be a successful big league manager."

Shapiro also dreaded what was coming in 2003, and he knew that he needed a manager who bought into the plan that began with the 2002 trades.

"I wanted a guy who would be at his best when the bullets are flying and things are at their worst," he said. "Eric is at his best when everybody has doubts and everybody questions what you're doing. In this game, there is so much negativity, so much failure. It would be so easy to compromise."

Shapiro also knew that some veteran managers would say all the right things to the front office and even to the media—for the record. But privately, they'd tell some reporters how they had no chance to win, how the team was too young. Most of the time, this approach fails. The rebuilding plan falls apart because the manager is not committed to it. And the manager is fired because he doesn't win enough games or develop enough players. But managers often play the political Cover My Butt game with the media to protect their own reputations. So if it collapses, they say it was the fault of the general manager. If it works, then the manager can grab some of the credit.

Wedge refused to do this.

"He is uncompromising," said Shapiro. "I could rest easier because I knew this guy was going to take it as hard as I do when we lose, that he cares as much as I do and works as hard as I do—if not harder. He was going to move to Cleveland, be in the office twelve months of the year and be a part of our decisions. It's not what every GM wants in a manager, but it's what I want. I wanted him to be my partner. In the end, there is risk, but talking to Eric and from what I knew about Eric, I thought he was a good risk, the right risk for us."

Paul Dolan had several meetings with Wedge and was more impressed each time they talked.

"I was concerned that he had not at least been a big league coach," Dolan said. "But I just didn't think the lack of experience would be a big factor. He had been around the majors enough to know the drills. Everyone we talked to who knew Eric well told us that he had "major league manager" stamped all over him. I agreed with Mark that Eric could be a difference maker. But even if he didn't reach that level, having a minor league manager with a development background would work well for us. I knew he was a foxhole kind of guy, and we'd need that."

Shapiro paused as he thought back to the day when he knew he would hire Wedge.

"There comes a point where you take a risk," he said. "You want to minimize risk, but there always is some risk involved in every important decision. Talking to Eric, I believed he was capable of doing the things he said he could."

But there was a different type of risk for Wedge. He could not turn down the opportunity to manage in the majors. It might never come again to a guy with his background. He was a stranger to most baseball fans and owners, just another faceless minor league manager who was putting together a nice résumé.

"When I took the job, I had to respect the fact that this might not work," said Wedge. "Or it might not work on the timetable. There were no guarantees."

He meant that there were no guarantees that he'd still be the manager when the team began to win, assuming it did.

"While 2002 was tough, because of all the trades, I knew that the full wrath of the moves would not be felt until 2003," said Wedge. "I knew it would take a lot of strength, a lot of toughness, and I had to be consistent as hell to be at my best on the toughest days.

"Fans were used to what happened [in the 1990s]," Wedge said. "The payroll was going to be different. The players were different. Everything was different. We were going to open ourselves to a lot of criticism, the arrows would be coming from all over the place. I knew that when Mark said he wanted to contend in 2005, we had no map to work off of. We were blazing a new trail. No turnaround had ever been made that fast."

Not by cutting the payroll by more than 65 percent, as the Indians did between 2001 and 2003.

Wedge's first move was to hire Skinner as third-base coach. This was also unusual, because Skinner had been the manager the year before—and had done nothing to lose the job. It might have seemed best to let Skinner find another job. Skinner might have felt rejected and looked to another team for a coaching position.

"The amazing thing was, the first call I got to congratulate me about getting the job was from Joel," said Wedge. "In spring training [2002], Joel and I drove to the ballpark together every day. I know him. I trust him. I wanted him by my side."

Skinner's family lived in the Cleveland area, and he didn't want to move his wife and four children for another coaching job. So he accepted Wedge's offer. A few months later, his wife was diagnosed with breast cancer. Joel and Jennifer Skinner are people of deep faith, and both believe it was a blessing for Joel not to get the job—so he could help Jennifer and the children during her cancer treatments. It was much easier for him to leave the team for a few days here and there as a coach than as a manager. (Jennifer Skinner has since been pronounced cancer free.)

Another good move was the hiring of Buddy Bell in 2003 to help Wedge. The idea came from Shapiro, who had made Bell an advisor in 2002 after he had been fired as manager in Colorado. Shapiro wanted an experienced baseball man with Wedge, and Wedge quickly embraced the idea of adding Bell to his staff.

"I was honored to have him," said Wedge. "He was my right hand. I'm a strong personality. I need a strong personality with me. On my most stubborn days, Buddy would not back down if he believed I was wrong. He was very good at telling me to slow down, to take each decision, each day, one at a time."

But Wedge was not just a Shapiro yes-man. Shapiro wanted Mike Brown to be the pitching coach. In the middle of his first spring training, Wedge went to Shapiro and said it wasn't working with Brown. He believed his former minor league pitching coach, Carl Wills, would be a better fit. Shapiro didn't like the idea of replacing Brown, but he agreed to it. Very few rookie managers would have had the self-confidence to demand the pitching coach be replaced in spring training, because they would know it was going to upset the bosses and reflect poorly on them. Wedge didn't care. He was sure he was right, that Wills was a better fit for his team.

Shapiro also went along with Wedge when Wedge wanted to fire hitting coach Eddie Murray in 2005. Murray was a close friend of the Shapiro family. Mark had known Murray for decades—his father, Ron Shapiro, was Murray's agent. Murray had been the hitting coach since 2003. It seemed silly to fire him early in 2005 because the team was slumping, but it was obvious that Wedge and Murray had communication problems. Wedge pushed for the change, and once again, Shapiro reluctantly agreed.

Shapiro realized that if he wanted a strong-willed manager, then he would have to deal with some of these issues concerning coaches. Wedge wanted his own guys.

"At the end of [each] season, the Indians usually brought up some of their minor league managers and coaches to be with the big league team in September," said Tom Hamilton. "Most of the guys were just glad to be on the chartered plane, eating the good food, enjoying the big league atmosphere. But Eric and Carl Wills would be up front in these serious discussions. It's not like they were trying to impress anyone or get their jobs, but you had a sense that they were thinking, 'When we get a chance to do this . . .' Eric was very serious. He was a man with a goal and plan to be a big league manager."

Wedge thought about things that many young managers don't—like how he looks to the players and fans when in the dugout.

"I had managers who went ape when a guy made a mistake," he said. "You start throwing things and that just shows up a player. Or when a pitcher gives up a home run, the manager pops out of the dugout and is out to the mound almost before the ball goes over the wall—his hand is out, and he's ranting and raving. That doesn't prove anything."

Wedge often seems stoic in the dugout, his face a brick wall, his chin jutting out. About all he shows is a few twitches.

"I know that fans want to see a manager yell at the players," he said. "But it's not appropriate to yell at a guy in public, unless they don't give you a choice and they come at you first. I do yell at my players, but I'll do it to the team in the clubhouse, or I'll take a guy in my office and do it in private. When a guy drops a ball, fans want you to blow up. But the guy didn't *want* to drop the ball. I don't believe in embarrassing people. I talk about respecting the game—part of that is respecting the players. I don't care if it's baseball, at the office, in a classroom, or anywhere else—no one likes being shown up. You do need to confront people, but have enough respect to do it to them in private."

Early in his rookie managerial season of 2003, Wedge was ejected from a game and watched the rest of the game from his office. He was shocked at how often the camera was on Buddy Bell, who was filling in as manager. That made him even more careful about not allowing his emotions to rule in the dugout. He didn't want to be seen throwing equipment around when a pitcher walked a hitter, and then have the player's wife or friends tell him what they saw the manager doing in the dugout while he was struggling.

Veteran *Akron Beacon Journal* baseball writer Sheldon Ocker often says that Wedge never seemed like a rookie manager. It was almost as if he began preparing for this job from the moment he played Little League. He seems to think before he says or does anything. He refuses to be caught up in the daily controversies that pop up during the baseball season. He'd rather eat a live rat and wash it down with Drano than criticize a player or management in public.

Often, he doesn't say much at all—at least to the media. His press conferences can be agonizing. He offers little insight. His favorite phrase is "Let's see how that plays out." He'll talk about "having to separate" one game from the next, even one inning from the next. He's never rude, he's just on message and not about to budge. You can ask him the same question four different ways—and get the same cryptic response. He would be a perfect spokesman for the Pentagon because military secrets would always be safe with him.

"I assume players will read or hear everything that I say,"

he said. "I want everything I say to have a positive effective on them—or to expedite their development."

Yes, Wedge did use the word expedite, something that most baseball managers would probably think is a foot disease.

Tribe media relations director Bart Swain said, "The players love how Eric handles this part of the job. He doesn't hammer them in the media. He's great in the dugout. He doesn't say anything in his postgame press conference that would lead the media to confront a player with a tough question and cause problems. He protects them, and the players appreciate that."

Even if it frustrates some media members and fans.

"I know that you know what's going on," he said. "I know that when I'm asked a question, I sometimes just don't answer it. In that respect, I'm like a politician. I do it on purpose. Like in 2003, I had reporters continually asking me if the real goal of the season was developing players. Of course it was, but I couldn't say that during the year. I had to keep saying, 'Hell, no, we want to win games.' We did, but I also had to develop players, and that meant playing young guys and sticking with them when they made mistakes. For example, we stuck with Casey Blake early in 2003 when he was in a real slump. If we had to win right now, maybe I don't go that long with him. But I believed in Casey, and after a while, he began to come through. It was like that with a lot of our guys. I'm not going to name names in the press. I'm not going to jump on a guy, throw him publicly to the wolves. I don't care how many times people ask me about it, I won't do it."

Wedge is almost anal about not wanting to appear that he's looking for any credit. He barely mentions any of his strategies that work, and quickly takes the blame for those that backfire. He wants the attention on the players, and makes it a challenge to write any sort of meaningful story about him.

Wedge spent much of a winter morning in an interview for this book, and the only question that seemed to catch him off guard was when I mentioned how he also has trouble praising individual players.

He demanded an example.

I recalled a day in late August of 2005 when I was writing a story about Victor Martinez, who was leading all of baseball in hitting after the All-Star break. He had carried the team for two weeks when Travis Hafner was hurt. He was catching every day. The guy was tremendous.

Wedge said, "Victor is doing a really good job for us."

He would not elaborate.

I asked if there was a problem with Martinez, a reason he refused to throw him a few verbal pats on the back.

"No," Wedge said. "The guy was playing great."

So what was the problem with just being nice?

"I think it goes back to how I grew up," he said. "I was taught never to get too high or too low. I was not given a lot of praise. It was like you want to keep everything at an even keel."

"Nothing wrong with gushing a bit when it's earned," I said.

"I'll think about it," he said.

It's too early to tell if Wedge will become an elite manager, the "difference maker" Shapiro sought. He was the ideal choice for the Indians during the rebuilding period. In his first two seasons, he endured some very bad baseball and even worse relief pitching.

Occasionally, Shapiro sounds frustrated about dealing with one of baseball's tightest budgets. He sees moves that he'd like to make, only the dollars aren't there. He sees moves that he's made strictly because they were all the team could afford—and as with some bargain basement shopping, it didn't take long for things to break down.

Wedge is the one who has to live the moves every day. He had to try to make a bullpen work in 2004 when Bob Wickman was hurt. He was forced to rely on Jose Jimenez, Scott Stewart, and Mark Wohlers. He had to turn career minor leaguer Casey Blake into a starting big leaguer at third—then in right field. He had to be patient as veteran third baseman Aaron Boone came back from two knee surgeries. He had to know that Shapiro could not just pick up the phone and buy a starting pitcher or heavy-hitting outfielder. In his first two years, it was remarkable how Wedge refused to even bend, much less break under the pressure of losing and the crazy quilt of a roster. That was especially true in the first half of 2004, when the Indians had the worst bullpen in baseball and lost game after game in the late innings. Nothing can destroy the morale of a team faster than heartbreaking, ninth-inning losses. They make a manager look like an idiot, because he keeps turning to a closer who just opens the door on more trouble. They make the starting pitchers strain a little too hard to finish games, because they have no confidence that their lead (and victory) will be preserved. They make the hitters begin to mistrust the pitchers, seeing all their good work at bat wasted.

Wedge was able to break in young players such as Travis Hafner, Grady Sizemore, Cliff Lee, Jhonny Peralta, Martinez, and Blake. Under Wedge, Jake Westbrook established himself as a 15-game winner. Veterans Scott Elarton and Kevin Millwood revived their careers (then left the Tribe via free agency). He got more mileage out of the streaky Ben Broussard than many baseball people believed was possible.

"Eric was at his absolute best when it seemed that everybody had questions, everybody was doubting our plans," said Shapiro. "The players never once saw any pressure, any fear, from Eric. There is so much uncertainty, so much failure in baseball, it's easy for things to go negative and undermine a clubhouse. Eric would not allow that to happen."

That's why Shapiro has twice extended Wedge's contract. He

really believes they are partners, so both should be signed up for the same length of time. Many managers take much of the winter off and don't live in the city where they work. Wedge, on the other hand, is more like an NFL coach. He is in the office nearly every day, in season and out of season. He takes part in all the key decision-making meetings. He helps Shapiro sketch the big picture of how the team should be run. It's very different from the John Hart era, when it was Hart who drew all the lines in ink—and Hargrove was there to color inside Hart's boundaries. Hart made all the major decisions on trades, free agents, and minor league call-ups. He even imposed his will on Hargrove's coaching staff, sometimes firing men whom Hargrove liked. Hargrove had a knack of sometimes talking Hart out of impulsive moves. He also was superb at blending different personalities into a team that usually played well together. But Hargrove never had the same influence as Wedge does with the front office. Hart also tended to keep Hargrove on a short string in terms of his contract, often waiting until the final year to grant an extension. No one would have dared consider them partners in any sense of the word. To be fair to Hart, his system was successful, and it's still the most common mode of operation. Hart also had been a minor league catcher, a minor league manager, and a big league coach before moving into the front office.

"I'm not an ex-player or an ex-coach," said Shapiro. "I need my manager to be my complement in the clubhouse, an extension of my beliefs and standards. He is the guy executing our plan."

Hargrove has been impressed by Wedge's preparation and dedication.

"When I first met Eric, my only concern was that he'd burn himself out by midseason," said Hargrove. "He was working so many hours. But he has learned to back off a little. As for the rest, he knows how to relate to players and he does a good job handling the game. He doesn't make many mistakes."

In 2005, Wedge's team staggered at the start for the third con-secutive season. They rallied in the heat of the summer, and were in position to win a wild card playoff berth until the final week-end of the season. But his team lost five of six games, and he was criticized for being too rigid, too by-the-book as a manager. He consistently issues the fewest intentional walks in baseball, and saw some games lost when pitching to the likes of Manny Ramirez and Mike Sweeney with a base open and a lesser hitter on deck. His team also had a 22–36 record in one-run games, which some blamed on their inability to bunt. It probably had more to do with a strong pitching staff that kept every game close, especially the bullpen, which dominated the late innings. It also was the product of an offense that could be powerful but very streaky. His team won 93 games, more than anyone expected. Yet it failed to just play .500 ball in the final six games at home, when that was all they needed for a postseason appearance.

Like his players, Wedge is still learning. While he won't pub-licly second-guess any moves he made down the stretch, he joined the rest of the front office in studying every one-run game in 2005, trying to figure out what went right—and wrong.

"I don't worry about losing my job," he said. "I learned that a long time ago. If you worry about keeping your job all the time, you really won't do your job well. You won't do what is best for the team. I love to manage. I love the responsibility. I love to watch our guys play, and I appreciate how they have grown as a team. This is all I've really wanted to do for a long time."

CHAPTER 10

"DO YOU WANT TO STAND FOR SOMETHING?"

VISION AND VALUES

The first time I heard about the Indians' new "vision statement," I yawned. So did most of my colleagues in the media, at least those who weren't making jokes about it.

You can find it on the walls of the offices where Mark Shapiro and Eric Wedge spend much of their time. They'll tell you that they take it seriously, even if no one else does.

> CLEVELAND INDIANS VISION STATEMENT:
> To build and sustain a championship-caliber team that competes passionately, relentlessly and professionally. And in the process, make a positive statement about its collective vision and core values.

The Indians came up with this after the 2002 season, after trading off most of the veterans, writing off the season, and generally telling everyone that there wouldn't be much fun until 2005—assuming everything went right. They were going to "build and sustain a championship team" when Bartolo Colon and Chuck Finley were traded for some minor leaguers? When Manny Ramirez and Jim Thome had left town in the last two years? When Karim Garcia was hitting fifth? When the payroll had been slashed from $96 million in 2001 to under $50 million in 2003?

No one was buying it, at least in the media. The only reason the vision statement wasn't openly mocked more in public is that when most of us read it, we knew Mark Shapiro believed it. Even those who thought Shapiro wasn't equipped to revive the Tribe because he lacked the experience of a professional player or manager never doubted the man's character. He had been in the front office since 1992. He had earned a reputation as a hard worker and a straight-shooter, not a self-promoter. But while his vision statement was sincere, it definitely seemed unrealistic in the harsh, bottom-line world of professional sports.

"I knew that no one was going to stand up and cheer because we had a vision statement," Shapiro told me. "Let's face it, fans and the media just care about the results. They care about winning, not how you get there."

But with the team headed for the darkest days since the lights went on at Jacobs Field in 1994, Shapiro believed there was only one way for the Indians to return to winning. He knew the doubters would multiply, the criticism would mount, the losses would pile up. It was going to take extremely strong and committed leadership to withstand the public relations storm already shaking the faith of many around the team. That's why Shapiro had called a meeting of his most important people, gathered them all in one room, and asked them to ask themselves this question: "What do we stand for, what do we believe in?"

To most baseball people and fans, this would seem like a waste of time. The team is bad and it's getting worse. How about finding a way to get better players? How about buying some free agents? Now that's something worth meeting about, not a vague, feel-good notion such as a vision statement.

"We needed to agree on the things and values that bonded us together," he said. "We were building a team and needed a vision of what kind of team we wanted to build. I wanted to verbalize it to everyone in the organization, so we'd all be on the same page.

We come from different parts of the country, even different countries. We come with different backgrounds and experiences, different cultures and skill sets. But we were going to come together and agree that these are the values that drive our organization."

When Shapiro talks like that, it sounds like he's reading from the latest best seller on leadership. And Shapiro does read a lot of those books. But he had thought about this for years. He sensed that some teams actually had a vision statement; they just didn't know it. He grew up in Baltimore with the Earl Weaver Orioles. His father, Ron Shapiro, represented many of the team's stars, including Eddie Murray and Brooks Robinson. The Orioles consistently contended. They consistently were considered a class organization. They consistently pitched well and had solid fundamentals. They consistently produced quality players from their farm system. They consistently referred to their system as "the Oriole Way," even if no one ever bothered to write down exactly what the Oriole Way *was*. You knew it when you saw the team on the field.

"The Indians had gone from building a team through the farm system [in most of the 1990s] to assembling players from all different organizations, often getting them in the middle or late in their careers," said Shapiro. "We were just trying to maintain winning, but in the process we lost our identity. What did we really stand for? What is the 'Indian Way?' It became winning, just short-term winning."

Actually, the 1995 Indians were built the same way as Shapiro was rebuilding the current Tribe, only now there were no big-name free-agent acquisitions like Dennis Martinez, Eddie Murray, and Orel Hershiser.

The 1995 Indians had significant homegrown players: Charles Nagy, Manny Ramirez, Jim Thome, Julian Tavarez, Chad Ogea, Herb Perry, and Albert Belle. Several key players came from other teams' farm systems: Carlos Baerga (Padres), Sandy Alomar (Padres), Paul Sorrento (Twins), Kenny Lofton (Astros), and Omar Vizquel (Mariners).

The deals bringing Alomar, Lofton, Baerga, and Sorrento to the Tribe were much like the trades made by Shapiro that brought Grady Sizemore (Expos), Cliff Lee (Expos), Travis Hafner (Rangers), Casey Blake (Twins), Ben Broussard (Reds), and Coco Crisp (Cardinals).

The Indians of the middle and late 1990s were built on the same small market strategy that Shapiro was now using—the only difference being the veteran free-agents, Martinez, Murray, and Hershiser.

Now, consider the 2001 Tribe, which made the playoffs. Here was the usual starting lineup:

CF Kenny Lofton
SS Omar Vizquel
2B Robbie Alomar
RF Juan Gonzalez
1B Jim Thome
DH Ellis Burks
LF Marty Cordova
3B Travis Fryman
C Einar Diaz

Of that group, only Diaz and Thome were products of the Tribe farm system. Vizquel and Lofton could trace their roots to the Tribe of the middle 1990s, but Lofton actually was gone for a year (1997), then returned as a free agent. Those nine players represented seven different organizations. The starting rotation was Bartolo Colon, C.C. Sabathia, Dave Burba, Chuck Finley and a cast of thousands trying to be the fifth starter. Colon and Sabathia came through the Tribe farm system. This team had a lot of big names and a $96 million payroll. It won the Central Division with a 91–71 record, and was knocked out of the playoffs in the first round by Seattle.

If Indians fans have any memories of that Tribe team, they probably are rather vague. Just another good team that seemed to fall short when it mattered the most. As I was writing this, I forgot that Cordova and Burks even were with the Tribe until I checked the statistics from 2001. This was a team bought with big money to win now. Only Colon and Sabathia would have been considered possible stars on the rise. Thome and Vizquel were in their primes. Most of the others were nearing the end of their careers. Playing in a rather lame Central Division, the team should have won more than 91 games. It certainly had better talent and far more experience than the 2005 Tribe, which won 93 games and missed the playoffs.

If you keep spending $96 million, you probably can keep assembling teams that win close to 90 games. But, as Shapiro noticed, it was a team that was more about maintaining than building something. It's a heartless, mercenary approach that probably will never lead to anything more than a quick playoff appearance and then demand even more money for more free agents.

"When you watch your team play and win, you want to feel good about what you see," said Shapiro. "As a man, do you have a code? How fulfilling is it when you win? It's a personal choice. Do you want to win just by collecting talent, or do you want to stand for something?"

> SCOUTING MISSION STATEMENT:
> To scout in a passionate, relentless and systematical manner in order to provide accurate evaluations to assist in procuring championship-caliber Cleveland Indians players.

Shapiro doesn't often talk about this in public because he understands that it's irrelevant to most fans. But it matters to him.

One of his close friends is Scott Pioli, general manager of the New England Patriots. They often talk about what it takes to build a winner. Shapiro is a huge New England fan, not just because they win—but because of how they win. The Patriots consistently play together, with minimal distractions. They often overachieve. They generally play smart football. They rarely have the best overall talent in the NFL, yet they often have been the best team. That's because coach Bill Belichick and Pioli take into account the personalities of players before deciding if they are worth drafting and signing. They don't expect every player to belong on a church window, but they do believe character counts and that creating the right environment will carry you through the tough times that are a part of every season—the times that can tear some teams apart because the connection between team and teammates isn't strong. They are just mercenaries doing a job.

When asked about this subject, Pioli said that one of most important lessons that he and Belichick learned from their days with the Browns in the early 1990s is that they needed to draft "more pure football players, fewer projects and head cases." He said most players don't change their approach to the game from college or early in their careers. Handing a kid a couple of million dollars, then telling him that he'd better adjust his attitude is a mixed message. He has just been rewarded by being drafted and pocketing a massive signing bonus. Where is the motivation to change? New England consistently builds teams with a few stars and lots of dedicated, solid, smart, gritty players as a supporting cast. Belichick is a terrific coach, but he needs players who are willing to be coached.

You find these players by scouting for them—setting standards for the character expected of players, and not making major compromises. When Belichick was in Cleveland coaching the Browns, he brought in attitude-challenged players such as Andre Rison and Jerry Ball. He drafted on raw talent alone. There were no strict guidelines for scouting. New England has them now, and so do the Indians.

It does matter.

Talk to anyone who has dealt with pro athletes for an extended period, and they will tell you this: "You can't make these guys do anything."

As one frustrated minor league manager told me when he was assigned to work with Carlos Baerga in spring training, "The guy has a fundamental flaw in how he's fielding right now. Just about anyone can see it. But Carlos just won't let me coach him. There's nothing I can do but go out there and try again tomorrow. But I can't make him listen."

This was during Baerga's final spring with the Tribe in 1996, when he was heavy and full of himself after being a star on the 1995 World Series team. It also was the first sign that problems loomed for Baerga. By midseason he was traded, and he was never again the same player. After spending some time in the minors and even in Korea, Baerga has returned to the big leagues as a utility man—smarter, humbler, and in many ways, a true leader because he has learned from his mistakes.

You can only coach people who want to be coached.

That came to mind when I spent an afternoon with the San Antonio Spurs. It was obvious that star Tim Duncan has a close relationship with Coach Gregg Popovich. Duncan was a top pick in the NBA draft, an instant star and millionaire from the first day he stepped on a pro court. But he wants to get better. He wants to win. He has played on three championship teams, and he has allowed Popovich to push him, to teach him. That's how Duncan matured from good to great so quickly. Spurs general manager R.C. Buford told me, "Duncan just wants to win. He allows Pop to coach him because he knows that's what's best for everyone."

Popovich and Buford also talk to Shapiro. They helped train Danny Ferry, who was hired as the Cavaliers' general manager in 2005. Ferry and Shapiro became friends when Ferry played for the Cavaliers. Pioli, Ferry, Popovich, Buford, and Shapiro all consider themselves friends, and they brainstorm with each other. From these discussions, Shapiro continues to form his ideas of the best way to build a team. While successful organizations such as the New England Patriots and San Antonio Spurs talk a lot about these things, Shapiro took one step further and decided to put them in writing.

> PLAYER DEVELOPMENT MISSION STATEMENT:
> To develop true professionals, each of whom reaches his full potential mentally, physically, and fundamentally through a systematic approach founded upon Cleveland Indians' vision and values.

Shapiro knows that every professional athlete is driven by self-interest. In fact, so was his vision statement. Shapiro not only bought into it because he believed in these values, he was also sure it was the best way for the Indians to return to contention. But it had to be a vision that wasn't just his.. Every key member of his organization had to share it.

"I wanted to build with character and talent, and build from the farm system," said Shapiro. "Not only is it what I believe, but it's market driven. We aren't going to just be able to go out and buy veteran players each year on the free-agent market—not in Cleveland. So it made sense to try and figure out how to do it another way."

Some baseball people have compared the Tribe's approach to that of Oakland A's general manager Billy Beane, inventor of the Moneyball strategy made famous in the book of the same name by Michael Lewis. There are some similarities. Both teams rely on heavy-duty statistical data. Both are dealing with tight budgets and payrolls near the bottom of the American League. A key difference is that Beane goes strictly by the numbers, especially the OPS: slugging percentage plus on-base percentage. Beane also disdains drafting high school players, especially pitchers. While Shapiro and his staff do genuflect at the OPS altar, they are not nearly as rigid as Beane. They also will pick high school players in the upper levels of the amateur draft. Shapiro seems to blend old-line baseball common sense with the hard data of the Moneyball disciples.

Where the two teams completely diverge is in the area of a player's character. If the numbers look good, Oakland usually will take guy, period. The A's proved that by acquiring Milton Bradley after he flamed out in Montreal, in Cleveland, and with the L.A. Dodgers. Yes, Bradley is volatile, the A's say, but he has a high OPS.

Nor would the A's do what the Indians did on a winter's day in 2002, when Shapiro assembled his management team—new manager Eric Wedge, assistant general managers Neil Huntington and Chris Antonetti, scouting director John Mirabelli, and minor league director John Farrell—to talk about a shared vision.

The oldest was Mirabelli at forty-two, the youngest was Antonetti at twenty-eight. Shapiro was only thirty-six, Wedge was thirty-five. Their major league experience was limited. Farrell had the most, with parts of seven seasons and a career 36–46 record as a pitcher. Wedge had small sips of big league coffee in 39 games spread over four seasons. Shapiro, Mirabelli, Antonetti, and Huntington never played pro baseball. Perhaps the fact that they were relatively young and none had been major league star players, managers, or executives made them very open to what Shapiro planned.

"I loved it," Wedge said about the vision statement. "We knew some people would bash it, just as some would bash the program. But Mark had the balls to lay it out there for everyone to see. He was saying, 'Here it is. Here's who we are, here's what we intend to do.' And he also was saying you can critique us along the way."

These guys were true believers.

There's a saying, "When you don't have a target, you never have to worry because you'll hit it every time."

These guys painted a target all right, complete with a bold bull's-eye and the steps needed to get there. They brainstormed, they challenged each other, they dug deep inside and asked, "What do I really think? What is at my core? What do I want to be about professionally, aside from just winning?" They also asked, "What makes a winner besides talent?"

"Passion" is one of Wedge's favorite words. Passion for the game. Passion for winning. Passion for your teammates. Over and over, he stresses these qualities. An Old Testament proverb reads: "The man of integrity walks securely, but he who takes crooked paths will be found out." That comes close to one of Wedge's own proverbs: "Let's see how this thing plays out." He preaches patience. He's convinced playing the game "the right way" will lead to the right results.

The vision statement has become their Ten Commandments, their Bible. When they feel they're losing their sense of direction, they look back at what they wrote that day. They sometimes challenge each other with it when major decisions have to be made.

Indians president Paul Dolan is very aware of the vision statement, and he endorses it, though perhaps not with the same fervor.

"This is Mark's way of managing the team, and it's very consistent with what Eric Wedge believes," he said. "I like it. But I would not be unhappy if we won with some guys who were not the greatest on the planet. It's better to have the kind of team that we do now, but it's still about winning."

A real test would come soon enough, when the short-term lust for winning clashed with the long-term values of the vision statement. It came in the person of Milton Bradley. And it prompted a passionate argument between Wedge and Shapiro, in which Wedge would ask, "Does this thing on the wall really mean anything?"

CHAPTER 11

"WHAT WILL IT SAY TO THE OTHER PLAYERS?"

THE MILTON BRADLEY DILEMMA

Mark Shapiro wanted Milton Bradley to make it. He really did. So did most of the Indians' front office.

Ever have a troubled friend or a struggling prodigal in your own family? There's part of you that loves him, part of you that wants to kill him. There are days when you think that he's finally starting to get it, and months when he seems utterly hopeless. When things are calm, and it's just you and him talking, it really seems like he's trying to change. He's saying all the right things. He's even doing some of them.

And you want to believe . . .

You tell yourself that he's still young.

You tell yourself that he's bright, he's talented, and there have been others who have seemed just as lost, just as self-destructive, yet somehow they grew out of it.

You tell yourself that you've spent all this time, put in all this work, you just don't want to give up on him.

You tell yourself all these things and more, but down deep, you know better. You have a sad, sinking feeling that you are lying to yourself.

That was the Indians with Milton Bradley.

In 2001, John Hart was still the Tribe's general manager, but he had announced early in the season that this would be his final year in Cleveland. He had trained Shapiro, and had allowed Shapiro to do much of the work of a general manager that summer. Hart went to the games, but was distancing himself from the daily grind of running the team, allowing Shapiro to grow into the job. Hart told Shapiro to pursue some trades, especially if he could find some young talent. Hart was very aware that the 2001 Tribe was aging and the farm system was hurting.

In June, Shapiro worked out a deal with Dan O'Dowd. They were friends—O'Dowd had been Hart's assistant general manager in the late 1990s, Shapiro right below as farm director. Now O'Dowd was general manager in Colorado, and Shapiro had moved up into O'Dowd's old position as assistant general manager with the Tribe. O'Dowd was shopping for an outfielder who could hit, and Shapiro knew the Indians desperately needed a young catcher. They talked, and it eventually led to the Indians sending talented but injury-prone Jacob Cruz to Colorado for Class AA catcher Josh Bard and Class AA outfielder Jody Gerut, who was out for the season because of knee surgery.

It wasn't a big deal to anyone else, but it was to Shapiro, primarily because it was his first. Hart quickly listened to the reasoning behind the trade, then approved it. When Gerut had a strong season in 2003, it appeared to be a steal. Bard had developed into a solid big league backup catcher. Cruz had bounced from team to team, unable to stay healthy or stay anywhere for long. Gerut eventually had knee problems and faded, traded away in the middle of 2005. In the end, like with most small deals, not much was gained long-term, except you'd much rather have a reliable defensive catcher like Bard than a player like Cruz.

The real deal Shapiro wanted to make in that summer of 2001 was for a center fielder. Shapiro knew Kenny Lofton was a free agent at the end of the season. He knew payroll cuts were coming (though he couldn't have imagined how deep they would be). He knew he needed a new center fielder for 2002.

"We targeted about six young center fielders," said Shapiro. "We had Terry Francona and our scouts go out and watch the best center fielders in the minors. We looked at Alex Escobar, Vernon Wells, Milton Bradley, and some others. We made attempts to trade for all of them."

Yes, the same Terry Francona who later would manage the Boston Red Sox to the 2004 World Series title. At this point, he had just been fired in Philadelphia and was hoping to manage elsewhere. The Indians wisely brought him in as a special advisor and scout.

Everyone who looked at Bradley loved his skills. A switch-hitter with above-average speed, above-average arm, above-average power, above-average defense in center field. The Indians saw Milton Bradley the way every team that scouted Milton Bradley imagined him.

IMPACT PLAYER!

FUTURE STAR!!

MIDDLE-OF-THE-DIAMOND POWER!!!

FIVE-TOOL PLAYER!!!!

And suddenly, word was that Bradley was available.

The Indians knew why. He had problems, lots of problems. He fought with managers, teammates, umpires. He didn't seem to trust anyone.

He had a little Albert Belle in him.

At least, that was the concise version of the attitude section of the scouting report. But the Indians had been the team that drafted, developed, and dealt with Albert Belle. That was back in 1987, when Belle was a star at Louisiana State University. No college player had more power. No college player had more baggage. Belle was an angry young man dueling with authority, be it his coaches or umpires. He had been suspended. He had scared some teams away. The Indians, desperate for young talent, picked him in the second round. He became a star. He was not much fun to be around—until the game started; then he produced. Did he ever produce. He hit home runs. He drove in runs. He scowled and growled and glared at the world, but he played every day. No one really liked Albert Belle except during games; then you loved him. He never gave away an at-bat, and he just kept getting better and better as a hitter. His home run totals from 1991 to 1996 were: 28, 34, 38, 36, 50, 48. He was never satisfied with any season. He lived to drive in runs, as his RBI totals for that same period show: 95, 112, 129, 101, 126, 148.

Albert Belle always wanted more.

More hits.

More home runs.

More RBI.

More money.

The Indians kept telling themselves that Belle was "getting better" with his off-field issues, but they knew they were conning themselves. He remained a hostile presence. Tribe fans know all the stories of his problems, and it really isn't worth dipping into the old foul-tasting stew—throwing balls at fans and photographers, cussing out reporters, smashing teammates' CDs, busting up parts of the dressing room. The Indians put up with it for one reason: Belle was perhaps the premier power hitter in the game. They compromised their values because they thought the payoff was worth it. Belle drove in runs and helped you win, and he played hurt and played every day. Just as you could count on Belle's temper flaring, you could bank on him refusing to miss games and driving in runs. The tradeoff was worth it until Belle became a free agent and wanted to become the highest-paid player in the game. The Indians backed away. He signed with the Chicago White Sox. The Indians never regretted either decision: taking Belle's outbursts along with his RBI, and letting him say good-bye when the price went too high.

•   •   •

Maybe Bradley would not be a long-term answer in center field. Maybe the Indians would only get a few years out of him. Or maybe they really could help the young ballplayer. In the summer of 2001, Bradley was twenty-three and had already been in the majors. He wasn't much older than some players drafted out of college. Montreal was willing to talk trade about Bradley because he had just alienated Expos manager Felipe Alou by refusing to run out a ground ball. He didn't seem the least bit sorry about it and was shipped back to the minors. This wasn't a surprise; Bradley had earlier been suspended in the minor leagues for an incident with an umpire. The Expos weren't going to give him away, but they no longer were sure that he'd be a star. As Shapiro talked to the Expos, he knew the risk. The Indians' director of player development, Neal Huntington, had been an assistant minor league director in Montreal when Bradley was the Expos' second-round pick in the 1996 draft, and during the first three years of Bradley's minor league career. Huntington also had a psychology degree from Amherst College. Like most people who spend time talking to Bradley, Huntington liked Bradley. But he also knew of the trouble spots. Indians' assistant general manager Chris Antonetti had also worked in the Montreal farm system in the late 1990s when Bradley was there.

There were no secrets about Bradley. The Indians knew his talent, and knew his troubles. But they also thought they could help him. They had people who knew Bradley, people who wanted Bradley to succeed.

Here's how it works with a player like Bradley: You can talk yourself into taking him, or you can talk yourself out of it. In the end, the question is if you think he'll be worth all the grief that you know will be coming.

"We had confidence in our support system [for players]," said Shapiro. "We had the right resources here, and *if* there was a chance—and you knew there might *not* be a chance—but if there was a chance to help this guy as a human being and as a person, we were a good place to nurture and support him."

Each of Shapiro's words is genuine. The Indians take what Shapiro describes as a "holistic" approach to developing their players. They have a staff psychologist. They have a battery of medical trainers, physical conditioning people, experts to help with diet and any other personal issues. If Bradley were to thrive, Cleveland could be the place. At least, that was Shapiro's thinking.

The Expos asked for Zach Day, a right-handed pitcher who reminded former Tribe manager Charlie Manuel of Charlie Nagy. The Indians had picked up Day along with Jake Westbrook for David Justice. That was in 2000, when the Yankees were desperate to get back to the World Series and willing to trade top prospects for a player who could help them right away, even one like Justice with a lot of miles and a long list of injuries. It really was a good deal for both teams, as Justice made an instant impact in the Yankee lineup while Day and Westbrook were maturing in the Tribe minor league system. In the summer of 2001, the Indians were sure both could eventually start in the big leagues. At the time, Day was 9–10 with a 3.10 ERA at Class AA Akron and had just been promoted to Class AAA Buffalo, where he allowed one run in six innings in his first start. He was a twenty-three-year-old right-hander with a superb sinker.

"I was sitting there knowing how we all liked Day," said Shapiro. "Eric Wedge had managed Day in Akron [in 2000] and felt strongly about Day as a pitcher and a guy. Eric had also seen Bradley and liked Milton's talent. But I was sitting there with this deal pending, Day for Bradley. My staff loved Day, loved his makeup, and to a man they were convinced he'd pitch in the majors. But we had a glaring hole in center field and we needed something to build upon. We needed young position players in the upper levels of the minors. That's why I had already traded for Gerut and Bard."

This was Shapiro's first major decision as GM-in-waiting. He wanted to talk to Montreal about some trade possibilities other than Day, but Expos general manager Jim Beattie told him, "You have thirty minutes. We have another deal pending for Bradley. If I don't hear from you, I'm taking it."

Shapiro and his staff believed Beattie. Most of baseball knew the Expos were ready to move Bradley, and several teams were interested in him for the same reasons as the Tribe—he had enormous talent. And this was the final day before the end of the summer trading deadline. Bradley would not be with the Expos by midnight, and Shapiro could feel the pressure of the clock tick . . . tick . . . ticking.

In the room with Shapiro and his scouts was John Hart, who had been mostly a quiet observer. Shapiro looked at the man who had been his mentor, the man who was the reason he now sat in the decision-making chair.

"Mark, it's your call," said Hart.

Hart had been willing to take a risk with troubled players. The one trade he did make during the 2001 season—and he made it over the objections of Shapiro—was shipping Steve Karsay to Atlanta for John Rocker. Rocker was a mental mess after his rambling, politically incorrect interview with *Sports Illustrated*, in which he seemed to attack virtually every minority group. Once a premier left-handed pitcher, he was still throwing 95 mph but had no idea where the ball was going. He was heckled in every ballpark. In a sport where whites are often a locker room minority, considering the immense influx of Latino players, Rocker was viewed with suspicion by some of his teammates. They wondered, "If this guy is willing to say all these racist things to *Sports Illustrated*, then what does he really think?" Rocker was 3–7 with a 5.45 ERA for the Tribe. He divided the dressing room: many players resented not only that good guy Steve Karsay had been traded for Rocker, but that management then wanted Rocker to close at the expense of the highly respected Bob Wickman. The deal was a disaster, but Hart took the chance because he loved Rocker's rocket of an arm, and he disregarded everything else about this troubled, sometimes paranoid soul.

So Shapiro had a pretty good guess what Hart thought. If he was willing to throw the dice on Rocker, why not Bradley? The kid certainly couldn't be any worse. This was a Hart-type deal. No one thought Day would become an All-Star, but that possibility was real for Bradley.

"This ran counter to my instincts because of the makeup of the players," said Shapiro. "But we had that huge hole in center, and this is a very hard asset to acquire."

So Shapiro made the deal.

Bradley came exactly as advertised, talented but temperamental. The question was, which part would rule? Would his talent overcome his temper? Would he, like Belle, be worth the trouble? Could he develop not just as a player, but as a person?

Milton Bradley came from a fatherless home in the inner city. He was raised by a strong mother. He was told to take care of himself, not to get close to many people because they wouldn't be there for him when it mattered. He wanted to have close relationships yet seemed to work hard at pushing people away.

More than once, Bradley told me, "It's hard for me to talk to strangers. It's even harder to trust people. I don't know if I'll ever trust people . . . My mother always told me that I had to stand up for myself," he said.

He wanted instant respect and was angry when he didn't receive it. He believed most people were against him. He was sure that no one understood him, or even wanted to make a real connection. He was determined to live his own way, even if it made life harder.

"I've always lived on the edge," he told me. "If they told me to be there at 5:15, I showed up at 5:14. If I was supposed to run to first base in 4.0 [seconds], I might run 4.0 once or twice, then do a 4.2."

Sometimes he was just a little late, as if to prove a point. He did it knowing it would cause trouble, making life harder for him. But he did it anyway, rationalizing that the self-inflicted grief was worth it. H. G. Wells once described a character in one of his novels as "not so much a human being as a civil war." That's Bradley, a man who is both very human and at war with himself.

Bradley wanted to set up his own rules. For example, he once told me that he hated "phony hustle." He meant guys sprinting to first base when they hit a harmless pop-up or a weak ground ball. No way would they be safe, so why make a big show of even trying? At least, that was his view. But occasionally, ground balls are muffed, pop-ups are dropped. Besides, baseball is not nearly as physically demanding as football or basketball, unless you happen to be a catcher or pitcher. Most hitters are asked to run hard ninety feet to first base an average of four times a game. Not exactly like doing a marathon in bare feet over a steaming cement pavement in July. So why not just hustle, phony or not? What's the difference? Besides, it makes the bosses happy. It also is the right way to play the game, according to purists such as Eric Wedge who believe there are certain standards that should be met. Bradley refused to buy into that code. He had little interest when Wedge and others talked about the need to "respect the game." He never believed the game (or its people) respected him. Baseball was something to be used for his benefit. That's how it worked in the streets. Get what you could out of any opportunity. You don't owe them anything, and they don't owe you.

Shapiro and Huntington were desperately trying to reach Bradley. He would promise to change, sincerely apologize, insist that he had learned from his mistakes—and sincerely mean every word that he was saying. And a month later, there would be another incident. You could have a long, meaningful conversation with him on Monday, when he was engaging and really seemed to think you were a friend. Then you'd see him a few days later, and he'd walk past you without a word, ignoring your friendly hello and not making eye contact. He often did this with his teammates and coaches, people who usually share an instant rapport because they are in the same profession, facing the same challenges.

"One time, I had a delightful conversation with Milton," said Paul Dolan. "Several times after that, he would have just run me over in the hallway if I hadn't gotten out of his way. It was like I wasn't there."

Bradley was convinced that others were just waiting for him to mess up, that no one actually believed he could change. Certainly some people around him were in that category, primarily because they had counted on Bradley before and he had indeed let them down.

So when a problem arose, his immediate reaction was to lash out, embarrassed and enraged. When Bradley got what he thought was a bad call from an umpire, he didn't just think the umpire was wrong. This was a challenge to Bradley's manhood. The umpire thought he wasn't worthy of getting the same breaks on a borderline pitch that others received. Or perhaps Bradley guessed wrong, looking for a breaking ball on the outside corner and the pitcher threw a fastball right across the middle of the plate for a called strike three. Rather than just accept that he was wrong, he lashed out at the umpire for daring to call the third strike and making him look bad in front of his teammates and thousands watching in the stands. That's why Bradley threw his helmet and bat at one umpire. In another game, he went into the dugout and then heaved about a dozen bats onto the field. He has had moments when he needed to be restrained by teammates because it appeared that he would assault the umpire.

Other times, when Bradley made a mistake, he'd run. That

happened when Bradley was stopped for speeding in the Akron suburb of Cuyahoga Falls. Instead of just taking the ticket, he sped away from the officer. He ended up appealing the case, and kept losing. He spent a weekend in jail, and then had to do community service. No doubt his legal fees cost him far more than just paying the speeding ticket.

Bradley told *Akron Beacon Journal* writer Sheldon Ocker, "I drive as fast as I want in California, and I never get a ticket. But I've been stopped five times in Ohio."

Then Ocker wrote, "Obviously, the fault lies with the state of Ohio. Bradley's native California understands him."

That's a funny, throwaway line by Ocker, but it probably has some truth to it. Bradley just wishes the world would see things his way, then everybody would just get along fine. Of course, life doesn't work like that, as Bradley and the Indians discovered.

After the purge of veteran players in 2002, Bradley was right in the middle of the 2003 rebuilding movement. Center field belonged to him. He was the most gifted player among the Tribe's non-pitchers. He was coming off a 2002 season in which he batted only .249 with nine homers and 38 RBI in 109 games, but he also did two significant stints on the disabled list. The first was when he crashed into the center field wall chasing a fly ball, and the ball bounced off the wall and bashed into his eye, breaking a small bone. He healed, played for a while, then went down with an appendectomy.

In 2003, Bradley started healthy and strong. He hit in spring training, hit once the season began, and seemed destined to hit like so many scouts believed he could. Bradley is six feet, 200 pounds, with an athletic ease and grace as he patrols center field. He bats from both sides of the plate, and has a smooth, strong, compact swing. That season, he hit .321 with 10 homers, 33 doubles, and 56 RBI in 101 games. He consistently drew walks and had an outstanding .421 on-base percentage. He was angry at the All-Star break when he was hitting .338 but not chosen for the game. He believed that the people picking the team held his past problems against him. He believed the Indians didn't promote him enough. He believed he got a raw deal. He was not interested in the fact that this was the first time he'd really done anything in the major leagues. He was right, some people in baseball did question his attitude. He continued to battle umpires. He ripped the Kansas City Royals in a newspaper interview, and discovered that some of his teammates posted a sign reading SHUT UP AND PLAY in his locker the next day. He was benched by Wedge for failing to run out a ground ball, then yelling at the manager in the dugout.

"I saw Milton disrespect [hitting coach] Eddie Murray," said Tom Hamilton. "If you're going to disrespect Eddie Murray, that's a problem. Eddie was a great player and came from Los Angeles just like you . . . and you have so much in common . . . I saw this and thought Milton was just hopeless."

Remember, before the 2003 season the Indians came up with their vision statement, which stressed team play, unselfishness, integrity, passion, and discipline. It seemed Bradley was testing this every week, if not every day. The Indians talked to him. They counseled him. They listened to him. The only thing that really improved was his performance on the field.

Bradley missed 61 more games in 2003 with injuries to his hamstring and lower back. That winter, he had the problem over the speeding ticket. In the spring of 2004, he told everyone how he had matured and was taking a new approach to the game. But he seemed to sit out frequently with minor injuries. It was obvious that he didn't seem to think spring training was critical for him. Meanwhile, Wedge believed he was compromising too much with Bradley, and he was telling the front office as much.

Bradley was not changing; he was just doing a better job at telling everyone that he was a different person. The talked had improved, the walk was the same.

Wedge had managed Bradley for part of the 2002 season at Buffalo. They were together in 2003. Over and over, Wedge made it clear what was expected of Bradley—the same things expected of every player. Over and over, Bradley promised to try harder. Over and over, there were more of the same incidents, almost as if he was defying Wedge, daring him to really do something drastic. Some players had come to Wedge and asked why Bradley was allowed to have his own agenda, why the team tolerated his lack of hustle. Wedge would say they were working hard with Bradley and he was talented, so let's be patient. But Wedge had doubts anything would change.

Despite Bradley's successful season in 2003, Shapiro was worried. He and his staff had several conversations about Bradley. Shapiro was looking for bright spots. He was excited by what Bradley did when on the field. But down deep, Shapiro knew he was selling out, that for all the plans to develop an "Indian Way" as part of the team's vision statement, Bradley was not about to buy into those values.

Late in the spring of 2004, Bradley hit a short fly ball to left field during an exhibition game against Houston in Kissimmee, Florida. He thought the shortstop would catch it, and jogged to first base. The ball dropped into left field, and with reasonable effort Bradley would have been on second base. Instead, he was at first. When the inning was over, Wedge quietly went to Bradley, put an arm around him, and whispered that he needed to run out every ball.

"If he had just let it go, only two or three people in the dugout would have even noticed me talking to Milton," said Wedge. "I don't believe in calling a player out in public. But he exploded. I did the same thing to Milton that I've done to a thousand players in the past—talking to them without showing them up."

Bradley began screaming at Wedge, much as he did in the 2003 season when he was quietly reprimanded in the dugout for failing to hustle. Wedge yelled back. Bradley believed he was being picked on, because veteran shortstop Omar Vizquel didn't always run 100 percent on what seemed to be easy outs. Wedge said he didn't want to talk about Vizquel, and yelled back again. Bradley then stormed out of the dugout, changed clothes in the clubhouse, and left the team in the middle of the game, taking a cab back to his spring apartment.

"Lots of things had happened with Milton before that day," said Wedge nearly two years later. "What happened to Milton was a disappointment to me because we'd spent so much time on that young man. But lines had been drawn, and he crossed them."

That evening, Wedge met with Shapiro and Antonetti at Shapiro's spring home. Wedge said he felt he could continue to manage Bradley, but he'd have to compromise everything the organization said it believed. He said he needed to send a message to the rest of the team that this would not be accepted. Bradley had done the same thing in 2003. He had done this to other managers in the minors. Something had to be done.

"My immediate response was to play the devil's advocate," said Shapiro. "I said it was important not to react to things emotionally. And no, I was not ready to get rid of Milton."

Wedge countered, "If we turn the cheek on this one, what will it say to the other players?"

Wedge mentioned that they had sat down with Bradley and told him what was expected, and what would happen if he rebelled again. He was told they would trade him. Well, it had happened again. Now what?

Shapiro was thinking, "Milton is our best player, the most talented athlete by far, and we have been compromising and compromising with him. How long does that last? When does it stop? If you have guidelines, you can't have a completely different set of rules for someone else."

But Shapiro wanted to be sure. The team had invested so much in Bradley, not just in terms of dollars, but also energy and emotion. No player received more attention from the front office. He was just turning twenty-four—is that too soon to give up?

Wedge told Shapiro that if the team did nothing, "We could just take that thing off the wall."

He meant the vision statement, which was posted in the dressing room and so many other places.

"If we believe this, then we have to do something," said Wedge.

Shapiro knew the issue was much bigger than Milton Bradley. It went to the heart of what the Indians claimed they would become. They insisted they had to be different to be successful. Some other teams may be able to convince themselves that Bradley was worth the migraines, but that was beside the point.

Shapiro did not make a decision that night. He told Wedge that he needed to think about it. He talked to Paul Dolan, and the owner wasn't sure they needed to bail out on Bradley just yet.

"I usually don't get involved in trades, assuming there are no major financial considerations," said Dolan. "In fact, this one would probably save us money. Milton [$1.7 million salary] was likely to be traded for some minor league prospects. But it bothered me because we didn't have to do it. We were going to trade away our best player because of his character. We dealt with Albert Belle, why not Milton?"

That led to a discussion of why Milton Bradley was not Albert Belle. In his two full years with the Tribe, Bradley had missed 125 games because of injuries. He had shown flashes of stardom, but nothing like Belle. And if they traded Bradley, they had Coco Crisp to take his place.

"At this point, we had no idea what kind of player we had in Coco," said Dolan. "I would have been delighted if Eric wanted to give it another try with Milton."

Actually, many in the organization had Crisp pegged as a reserve outfielder. No one believed he had the same raw talent as Bradley.

While Shapiro never said as much in several interviews for this book, he had to be wondering, "What if I trade this guy and he becomes a star?"

That would be a nightmare. The Indians go through all the growing pains and anxiety with Bradley, then give up on him too soon. And who would be blamed for that? It wouldn't be Paul Dolan, Eric Wedge, or the players in the clubhouse who were worn out by Bradley's personality. It would be the general manager. Shapiro likes to say he doesn't worry about how his moves will be received by the media and fans. He just wants to do what is right for the Indians. No doubt, he believes that. But he is human. None of us likes to make a mistake that bounces back and haunts us. And things would be even worse for a young, unproven executive, like Shapiro was in the spring of 2004. About all that fans had seen from him so far was trading big names for prospects. His first major deal—the Robbie Alomar trade—was fizzling for both teams. Travis Hafner had yet to blossom into a star. Grady Sizemore spent the 2003 season in Class AA Akron. He looked promising, but there were still no guarantees about him or anyone else in the Bartolo Colon deal. And Colon did win 20 games in the 2002 season when he was traded by Shapiro.

Looking back now, it seems obvious that Shapiro had to move the troubled Bradley. But in the spring of 2004, trading Bradley was an even bigger risk than the initial gamble made in acquiring from Montreal. Now, the Indians *knew* Bradley could be a .300-hitting run producer if he could stay healthy and focused. Bradley was forcing Shapiro to really ask himself what was important, and what he really believed. Shapiro spent that night going over what had led to the vision statement. He thought about how he had said he was more like a "partner" with Wedge than a boss, and how they would make major decisions together. He knew they would not receive full value in return for Bradley, because baseball people would know the Indians had just become the second team—after Montreal—convinced Bradley was unmanageable. Part of Shapiro wanted to wait a little longer, see if this crisis would pass. Perhaps they could get a few good months out of Bradley, then maybe they could make a better deal for him. That course would have been embraced by ownership—always a wise course for a general manager. But Shapiro knew he had to support his manager.

Shapiro called Bradley and told the troubled outfielder that he was being assigned to Buffalo until a trade could be worked out. He told Bradley not to bother to come to camp; he was done with the Indians. He explained why. Then Shapiro announced to the media that Bradley was demoted to Buffalo, pending a trade. He said he had to back his manager, that "there is a line within which players can express their individuality. There's also a line they can't cross."

Within thirty-six hours, Bradley was traded to the Dodgers for two prospects—outfielder Franklin Gutierrez and pitcher Andrew Brown. Both spent 2004 at Class AA Akron while Bradley started in center field for the Dodgers.

"The way we handled this, we told the world that Milton was damaged goods," said Dolan. "But in the end, we believed it was important for the players to see us take some action, so I went along with the decision. After Mark came to Eric's way of thinking, I felt I could only push it so much. These are the guys we put in charge of the team."

The reason for the long story of Bradley's short tenure with the Tribe is to show how the team's management faced what really amounted to its first crisis of conscience in the Shapiro era.

It demonstrated that ownership was not going to impose its will on the baseball people. When it came to pure baseball decisions, it was up to Shapiro and his staff to make them. It also enabled Shapiro to endorse his manager.

"Eric was right," said Shapiro. "Not many jobs are like these, where you are around each other *every day* for nine months. You see each other *all the time*. The work environment means so much, you want it to be positive. The right work environment also can help us bridge the gap we have with some of the other higher-payroll teams."

Former Tribe manager Mike Hargrove served as a special advisor to the team in the spring of 2004, and he was impressed with how Shapiro handled the Bradley situation.

"I got to know Milton and liked him," said Hargrove. "We talked a few times in spring training, and he always was respectful, looked me in the eye, and you could tell that he was intelligent. But he got into it with a coach a few times, and that wasn't good. There were incidents that people didn't know about. This was before the thing happened with Eric. When I heard about that, they [the front office] asked what I thought—and I said they had to support Eric. Milton had to go. But I'm telling you, most general managers would not have had the guts to do what Mark Shapiro did. Very few would back their manager as forcefully as he did with Milton Bradley."

Dolan said, "I'm not saying we'll handle every situation like we did with Milton. If there is an Albert Belle who is out there every day and being productive and we have some problems, then we'll have to see. That will be a different bridge for us to cross."

Bradley did not turn into Albert Belle. Milton Bradley remained Milton Bradley. He had two stormy years with the Dodgers, where he continued to battle with umpires and management. He was suspended for five games in one incident. He also was hurt. He had some good months, but never could stay healthy for a full season. In 2004 and 2005, he batted .279, averaging 16 homers and 56 RBI. (Coco Crisp, surprisingly, turned out to be more productive for the Indians, averaging 15 homers, 70 RBI, and hitting .299 in that same span.) Bradley was then traded to Oakland after the 2005 season. Brown and Gutierrez worked their way up to the Tribe for a brief September stay in 2005, but they still have to prove they are viable big league players.

As for Zach Day, he's also fallen short of expectations. His best season was 9-8 with a 4.18 ERA in 2003 for Montreal. In the next two years, he had a 4-13 record. Now you can look back and wonder what all the fuss was about. None of these guys became stars. But the Indians did more than spend two years of turmoil with Milton Bradley—they found their soul.

CHAPTER 12

"THE FANS DIDN'T COME BACK."

THE END OF THE ERA OF SELLOUTS

Understand this about the Indians' 455-game consecutive sell-out streak: it will never happen again.

At least not in Cleveland.

It's always dangerous to write anything attached to the words *never* and *always*, because there *always* are exceptions—even to something that *never* seems likely to occur.

But the Indians will never sell out anything close to 455 games in a row again.

Here's how it happened.

The Indians had not been to a World Series since 1954. They had not been a serious contender late in the season since 1959. An entire generation of baseball fans grew up knowing only two things about the Indians: they lost, and they played in a big, old ballpark that was usually empty.

I still remember a fan who sat behind home plate and stood and clapped obsessively. We called him "The Mad Clapper," and his clapping echoed all over the park. So did the constant drumming of John Adams, far away in the center field bleachers—which seemed like they were across Lake Erie, up in Canada near the Arctic Circle. There was another guy who'd stand and scream, "WHO-LEE-OHH!" every time Julio Franco came to bat. It was so loud, John Adams heard it in the bleachers. Of course, at the old stadium, the left fielder could sneeze and the fans behind the plate would respond, "God bless you!" Most nights it was so quiet, you could hear the mosquitoes buzzing around the pitcher as he stood behind the mound, rubbing up the baseball.

While many older Tribe fans have warm memories of Cleveland Stadium, most would admit that the park was like a weird relative. You may like and understand him, but there are a lot of good reasons no one else does. The Stadium had those creaky wooden seats—many behind poles. Parts of the old cement concourse smelled like an animal had died once upon a time and no one could find the carcass. Restrooms backed up, sinks leaked, and paint peeled. No matter how many different renovations were attempted, nothing helped for very long. It was hopeless.

When the Indians moved into Jacobs Field in 1994, it was a stunning contrast, a major upgrade, a ballpark that was truly a field of dreams. Tribe officials said in the first few years of Jacobs Field, they'd see fans just standing and staring in awe at the park, the field, the scoreboard. Tours of Jacobs Field were popular. Fans often posed in front of the iron gates or the Bob Feller statue in front of Gate C, taking pictures of each other. You didn't see that at Gund Arena after it replaced the Richfield Coliseum as the home of the Cavaliers. Gund Arena didn't seem like that much of an improvement over the Coliseum. Many fans actually preferred the Cavs' old home. Very few Tribe fans would want to go back to the old Stadium.

You go from 1960 to 1993 with a bad team playing in a bad stadium, then suddenly things change. The Indians had assembled a core of young players in Kenny Lofton, Albert Belle, Carlos Baerga, Charles Nagy, Sandy Alomar, and Jim Thome, who were joined by two big-name veterans in Dennis Martinez and Eddie Murray, along with an unheralded shortstop named Omar Vizquel who was destined to win the hearts of most Tribe fans.

Here was the usual 1995 lineup and their All-Star appearances:

Kenny Lofton CF (6 All-Star games)
Omar Vizquel SS (3)
Carlos Baerga 2B (3)
Albert Belle LF (5)
Eddie Murray DH (8)
Jim Thome 3B (4)
Manny Ramirez RF (9)
Paul Sorrento 1B (0)
Sandy Alomar (6)
Dennis Martinez P (4)

Compare that to the usual 1989 lineup:

Oddibe McDowell LF (0)
Jerry Browne 2B (0)
Joe Carter CF (5)
Pete O'Brien 1B (0)
Cory Snyder RF (0)
Dave Clark DH (0)
Brook Jacoby 3B (2)
Andy Allanson C (0)
Felix Fermin SS (0)
Greg Swindell P (1)

Page back ten years to the usual 1979 lineup:

Rick Manning CF (0)
Duane Kuiper 2B (0)
Bobby Bonds RF (3)
Andre Thornton 1B (2)
Gary Alexander C (0)
Cliff Johnson DH (0)
Toby Harrah 3B (4)
Jim Norris LF (0)

Tom Veryzer SS (0)

Rick Wise P (2)

Now let's go back ten more years to the usual 1969 lineup:

Jose Cardenal CF (0)

Larry Brown SS (0)

Ken Harrelson RF (1)

Tony Horton 1B (0)

Russ Schneider LF (0)

Joe Azcue C (0)

Max Alvis 3B (2)

Vern Fuller 2B (0)

Luis Tiant P (3)

None of the players from 1969, 1979, or 1989 are in the Hall of Fame. Compare that to the 1995 lineup. Murray already is in the Hall of Fame. Thome, Ramirez, Belle, and Vizquel will receive serious consideration. Every member of the 1995 starting line except Paul Sorrento had made an All-Star team at some point in their careers. In 1989, only three players ever were All-Stars. In 1979, it was four players, and in 1969, there were three players. Some of these guys were All-Stars with other teams, but not with the Tribe.

Not only did the Indians have a ballpark the likes of which the fans had never experienced in Cleveland before, the 1995 team that played the first full season at Jacobs Field (remember, 1994 was cut short by the baseball strike) was more talented than anything most fans had ever seen in Cleveland.

A new ballpark, an All-Star cast, and the end of a long history of losing all came together to inspire fans.

But there was so much more. Consider the following:

• *The Browns moved to Baltimore after the 1995 season.* From 1990 to 1995, the Browns were 39–57 with one playoff appearance. Fans were waiting for a reason to cheer, and the Indians supplied it. As Tribe public relations vice president Bob DiBiasio said, "There was this huge, passionate fan base asking themselves, what should they do now that the Browns are gone?"

• *By the middle 1990s, the Cavaliers were stuck in mediocrity.* They had a rather boring team, as the Mark Price/Larry Nance/ Brad Daugherty era had come to an end. They played around .500 ball and weren't a factor in the playoffs. They had no star power. After 1993, they won only one playoff game heading into 2006.

• *The 1990s economy was strong, even in Northeast Ohio.* Usually, this part of the country is the first to go into an economic decline, the last to come out of it. Economic shock waves seem to hit harder and last longer here. But the 1990s was high tide for many fans, who had some extra cash to spend. They also didn't have to pay for Browns tickets.

• *There was a renaissance in downtown Cleveland.* The Flats and the area around Jacobs Field came alive with clubs, restaurants, and other businesses. It actually was cool to go downtown. In the 1970s and 1980s, Cleveland was like a city on life support, waiting for someone to pull the plug and put it out of its misery. Suddenly, the town was alive—and it seemed like a miracle! The Indians and Jacobs Field were the heartbeat.

• *Cable TV wasn't as big a factor.* In the middle 1990s, cable TV was not as powerful or lucrative for team owners as it is today. But a new ballpark was a huge advantage because so few teams had one. "Cleveland, Texas, and Baltimore were the three American League teams with new parks in the middle 1990s," said Assistant GM Chris Antonetti. "We could use the ballpark as a magnet to attract players because our park was such an upgrade over where most teams played." A new park in the middle 1990s also was a cash cow because of the revenue it produced from luxury suites and club seats. Ticket prices could be higher because the park was new and a good place to watch a game. A new Comiskey Park came to Chicago, but it was so boring, and the team so bland, it didn't help the White Sox. By the early 2000s, there were new parks everywhere from Detroit to Milwaukee to Cincinnati to Pittsburgh. It was no longer a novelty.

• *The new American League Central Division was less competitive.* In 1994, baseball owners realigned each league into three divisions. Dick Jacobs shrewdly volunteered to go into the Central. His marketing people wanted him to stay in the East, for more games with the New York and Boston, but Jacobs thought he'd have a better chance to win a title in a division that did not include the Yankees and the Red Sox. He was right.

• *Central Division spending was lower.* The Indians' Central Division rivals—Kansas City, Minnesota, and the White Sox—were not spending. Some years, the Tribe had double the payroll of the Royals and Twins.

All these things came together to enable the Indians, in the nation's sixteenth-largest TV market, to have payrolls in the top five in some of those seasons.

"We sold out the entire season *five* times before the home opener," said DiBiasio. "I'm talking *five years in a row!* That will never, ever happen again, because all these things will never, ever happen again here."

The sellout streak was critical because it brought in so much cash before the first pitch of spring training. That made it simple for the team to budget how much to spend for players. General manager John Hart put a premium on entertainment. He liked teams that hit. He liked big names. He wanted to put on a show for the fans. With big bats from Belle to Lofton to Thome to Ramirez, he did just that. The Indians didn't always play sound fundamental baseball, but they were so much fun to watch.

When it ended, it was like someone turned off the faucet.

By 2002, after all the changes, many Tribe fans had lost faith in ownership. They didn't care that the Dolans talked and acted much more like fans than Dick Jacobs ever had—at least early in their ownership. They just knew that from 1995 to 1999, the Indians ruled the Central Division, went to the playoffs every year, and had a lot of stars on the field. And now that had stopped. Tribe fans had suffered too many losses, too many free-agent departures (Thome, Ramirez, Kenny Lofton), too many stars traded, (Robbie Alomar, Colon).

Veteran Tribe fans are products of a dysfunctional baseball family. They grew up with decades of cheap owners, incompetent executives, and dismal teams. Now, when current general manager Mark Shapiro did something they didn't like, they started comparing him to Gabe Paul and Phil Seghi, who ran the team (some would say into the ground) during most of the 1960s, 1970s, and 1980s. Many of them don't even remember Seghi and Paul—they just remember hearing their fathers take those baseball names in vain. I know, because it's easy for me to fall into the same baseball depression. I wrote a book titled *The Curse of Rocky Colavito*, about the dark ages of Cleveland baseball that lasted nearly four decades. The book was published just as the team moved to Jacobs Field in 1994, and it's a long, sad story—sometimes funny in a twisted way—of how nearly everything went wrong. Fans of my generation loved it. These were their Indians, and they usually stunk.

Cleveland is a football town. The Browns can be the most inept organization in the NFL, but they still sell out every game. The expansion Browns were opening play in 1999, just as Dick Jacobs was selling the Indians. Seven years later, the Browns had compiled the worst record in the NFL for that time span. They had one winning season (2002) in those seven years. In the last three years, they were 15–33. By 2005, they were already on their third attempt to put together a front office/coaching combination. Overall, the Browns' report card since their return would at best rate a D, and that's being kind.

In the same period, the Indians had three seasons in which

they won at least 90 games, the last being a 93–68 record in 2005. Yet, during the winter of 2005–2006, the Indians received far more public criticism than the Browns. This is not to defend everything done by the Tribe, but it is a fact that Cleveland's baseball team has a far better track record under the Dolan ownership than the Browns have had under the Lerner family. But many fans simply don't trust the Indians. They have developed a fatalistic view that every good player will eventually leave, and they'll be replaced by another Chico Salmon, Alex Cole, Jamie Easterly, Alan Bannister, Miguel Dilone, and Gary Alexander.

When the Indians are winning big, Cleveland may be the best baseball town in the country, as the sellout streak demonstrated. But when the team falters, the fans are quick to turn away.

"The most surprising thing to me about 2005 was how the fans didn't come back," said Shapiro. "I know that we started slow, but by the middle of the summer, we were a strong contender for the playoffs. I didn't think we'd sell out every game like we did in the 1990s, but I never thought we'd have to work so hard just to draw 2 million. I just thought they'd come back faster once they saw what we were doing and that it was working."

Here's a measure of fan interest in the Tribe from 1999 to 2005:

Year	Season Tickets	Attendance	Payroll	Payroll Ranked	Revenue Sharing
1999	27,000	3.4 million	$72 million	9th	Paid $13.8 million
2000	27,000	3.4 million	$82 million	7th	Paid $12.8 million
2001	27,000	3.2 million	$96 million	3rd	Paid $12.9 million
2002	23,000	2.6 million	$78 million	14th	Paid $10.6 million
2003	15,000	1.7 million	$45 million	25th	Paid $4 million
2004	13,000	1.8 million	$39 million	27th	Received $4 million
2005	12,000	2.0 million	$45 million	26th	Received $4 million

The payroll rankings came from the Major League Players As-sociation. The season ticket totals and revenue sharing numbers are estimates that came from the Indians. Revenue sharing has a complex formula based upon an average over several years. That's why the Indians were still paying into the program in 2003, when they had the third-lowest attendance in the American League at 1.7 million. That was a 50 percent decrease from 2000, when they led all of the majors in attendance. Along with having the three highest payrolls in team history (2000–2002), the Dolans also paid $40 million during all of their ownership in revenue sharing, mostly because of the success of the Jacobs era.

The Dolans talked like fans during their earlier ownership days, not just setting the goal of winning more than one World Series, but promising to "spend when the time is right." (That promise was made in 2002, when the team was selling off its vet-erans, slashing payroll, and rebuilding.)

"The point my father was trying to make is he wanted to build a team," said Paul Dolan. "He didn't want to win a World Series like the 1997 Florida Marlins, then blow it up the next year. He wanted to sustain it. He wanted to put an organization together capable of putting together a championship-caliber team, year after year. St. Louis is the kind of franchise we had in mind. Does that mean you will go to three or four World Series in a row? That's not real-istic. He meant to say we want to build a team that can contend every year. His inexperience showed."

It also hurt the Dolans' credibility with the fans, especially when Florida tore everything down and still came back to win the World Series again in 2003. The Dolans were incredibly naive about the challenge of operating a franchise in the twenty-third largest population market and the sixteenth largest TV market in the country. (Fans in Northeast Ohio are upset when Cleveland is called a midsized market, but it's exactly that, according to rank-ings published by Northwestern University's MediaInfo Center.)

The Indians' new owners at first acted as if they planned to spend like the New York Yankees instead of the Minnesota Twins, a more realistic model. They wanted to please their new customers. Instead, this go-for-broke approach and a shaky start in the first few years wound up turning fans off.

"Fans fell in love with a group of players who could be counted upon to win the Central Division," said Paul Dolan.

When they bought a season's ticket in the 1990s at Jacobs Field, they knew they were buying into the playoffs. Fans liked the idea that the Central Division was their playground, even when the team was winning only 86 games, like in 1997. They knew they'd still go to the playoffs. Now, nothing is guaranteed.

Here's what happened to the Indians after 2001:

The Central Division improved. Minnesota became a strong, prospect-driven team in the early part of this decade, much as the Indians now hope to become. Then the White Sox began to grow and spend, pushing their payroll to more than $70 million in 2005, and over $90 million for 2006. Detroit and Minnesota were also outspending the Tribe by 2005. In the Jacobs Field glory years, the Indians often had double the payroll of the other Central Division teams. Now they could no longer buy their way to the top.

The novelty of Jacobs Field wore off. It was no longer a place to go simply because it's a nice ballpark.

The Tribe's support softened. When the stars left and the losing started, the fans stayed home. They went from perhaps the best baseball town in the country to one of the game's worst draws. This is baseball history in Cleveland. In 1948, they won a pennant and set an all-time attendance record. They did it again in the late 1990s (the difference being, the 1948 Indians also won a World Series). But look at how the team drew in the 1960s, 1970s, 1980s, and early 1990s. They usually were near the bottom of the league. Of course, they also had a lousy team in a terrible ballpark with usually inept front-office leadership. As a baseball town, Cleveland tends to run either hot or cold.

The economy got even softer. Cleveland lost so many major corporations to other areas of the country, and a few just closed. That meant a sharp decrease not only in the sale of season's tickets, but also luxury suites and loges. Those yield big money. In 2001, almost all of the 135 loges were sold. By 2005, it was down to 88. They sell for $40,000 to $180,000 each—and this is money coming in before opening day. The companies that used to buy these high-ticket nights out to entertain clients were disappearing.

Not only were the Browns back, but the Cavaliers suddenly became relevant. The Cavs caught the biggest break of any Cleveland sports team ever when they won the 2003 draft lottery and picked local hero LeBron James. Suddenly, they too were competing with the Indians for not just dollars from fans, but corporate support. And James attracts the kind of casual sports fan and businessperson who once frequented Jacobs Field when the Indians were the hot franchise.

The Dolans spent too much money too soon. They not only had the three highest payrolls in team history, they were stuck with paying $34.5 million in revenue sharing in their first four seasons. The money spent did not produce a big winner. That led to a decision, starting with the 2003 season, to spend only what they take in. They simply did want to—or could not afford to—lose any more money.

They paid too much for the team. The Dolans deny it, saying that given the state of the franchise—the winning, the sellouts— and their expectation of owning the team for a long time, it was not a bad investment. "I think the team is worth what we paid for it, given that we plan to keep it for a long time and the direction we now have the franchise going [after 2005]," said Paul Dolan. They paid more ($320 million) than it cost to buy the Los Angeles Dodgers ($311 million) at that same time. In a sport where there is no salary cap and where having a strong cable network in a large TV market is the key to financial success, it's hard to believe the Indians should have sold for more than another major league team. Even in a sport where nearly every owner eventually sells for more money than the original price of the franchise, the Dolans paid too much. It would be very hard for them to find a buyer offering even close to $300 million today for the Tribe, especially since teams like Cincinnati and Milwaukee have been selling for less than $250 million.

Cablevision stock dropped dramatically. Paul Dolan said the fall in the stock prices of Cablevision (the Dolan family business in New York) wasn't a major factor "because we had already bought the team before it fell. The franchise is owned by a series of family trusts (between the New York Dolans and the Cleveland Dolans), and the Cleveland Dolans have 100 percent control."

Since the Dolans took the team off the stock market and turned it into a private company after purchasing it from Jacobs, we don't have full, unbiased financial reports to check. But it's obvious from the high payrolls, the revenue-sharing payments, and the falling attendance that they have been losing a lot of money. They also increased spending on the minor league and scouting systems from $18 million to $25 million a year, putting them in baseball's top three investors in player development.

There also are credibility issues, at least in the eyes of some fans. Just as Shapiro's promise in 2002 to contend in 2005 seemed to follow him for three years, the Dolans' claim that they'll spend when the team is ready to contend is mentioned over and over by fans, who are still waiting for it to happen. Every time one of their own free agents leaves, another team's free agent turns down the Indians, or a veteran is traded for a younger player—fans criticize the Dolans. They say the Dolans are cheap. They say the Indians will never win. Even if they do have a strong season as they did in 2005, they won't be able to maintain it because of the Dolans.

"Spend when the time is right" is such a vague statement. What time is "right"? Spend how much? The Dolans never said, and that led fans to read into it what they wanted to hear—namely, the team would embark on a major spending spree when contention became a reality.

"That statement has always been misunderstood," said Paul Dolan. "The reality is, we spend what we take in. We don't try to make a profit. In reality, we spend what we make."

At times, the Dolans say things with the best intentions but end up leaving themselves open to criticism. That's why Dick Jacobs was smart to say so little.

"The goal is to not overspend in a manner that puts the franchise at risk," said Ken Stefanov, the team's senior vice president of finance. "It's risk/reward spending to what our revenues afford. If we do make a profit, it gets pumped right back into the franchise, either through the major league roster, player development, or improvements on Jacobs Field. The Dolans don't take any distributions of excess cash out of the franchise for their personal use."

"This is not a battle of owners' wallets, it's a battle of markets," said Paul Dolan. "New York and Chicago generate far more income than Cleveland and Pittsburgh. An owner may overspend for a year or two, but it rarely works. Within a few years, they are cutting payroll and trading off the free agents they signed."

In the last two years, the Dolans say they made a "slight profit" on the team—reportedly about $1 million annually. They say they put the money right back into the team.

"We have to develop our own players because we can't have an Alex Rodriguez, a Manny Ramirez, or a Jim Thome on our roster making what they do today," said assistant general manager Chris Antonetti. "Since 1985, no team has won a World Series with a player making more than 15 percent of the total team payroll. The Yankees can have a $30 million player because their payroll is over $200 million. This is all related to the size of the market."

In 2005, Ramirez earned nearly $20 million, which would have been 44 percent of the Tribe's $45 million payroll. Thome was at $13 million, which would have been 29 percent. Kevin Millwood was the Tribe's highest-paid player at $7 million—nearly 16 percent. As John Hart said, when the Ramirez bidding hit $180 million, "We are going to have the Manny Ramirez traveling show. We won't be able to put a team around him."

The Indians are trying to figure out what their real fan base is if they consistently contend.

"No one expects to sell out each game, like the 1990s," said Stefanov. "It seems that 3 million is unlikely, unless the team would reach the World Series. It could be about 30,000 a game—perhaps 2.5 million in a good year. Our next goal is to draw 2.5 million, to build back the fan base."

There's only one way to do that—get back to the playoffs. And with the new, tight budget, they'll have to do it the hard way.

CHAPTER 13

"A SENSE OF RELIEF"

THE TRIBE CONTENDS IN 2005

The Indians never should have won 93 games in 2005. They never should have been pressing the Chicago White Sox for the Central Division lead, nor should they have entered the final weekend of the season with a serious shot at making the playoffs as a wild card team. They also shouldn't have lost six of seven games to finish the season, missing the playoffs.

But the fact remains that the plan the Indians committed to in the middle of the 2002 season worked. Shapiro's prediction they would contend in 2005 was proved correct. Their batting average in picking prospects was excellent, their trades were mostly successful. They went from a team with a $96 million payroll to a $45 million payroll, and they were still in the game. When most teams need seven to ten years to rebuild and then contend, the Indians did it in three. That's why Shapiro was voted baseball's 2005 Executive of the Year by his peers. It's why his assistant Chris Antonetti was asked to interview for four different general manager jobs at the end of the season—and Antonetti had just turned thirty.

The point of all the moves starting in 2002 was not just to throw together a contender for one year, but to build a team capable of winning at least 90 games for several seasons. To do that, the Indians not only had to get better, they had to get younger and cheaper to keep some of their players around, just as they did in the middle 1990s.

In many ways, Travis Hafner turned into Jim Thome. Like Thome in his prime, Hafner walks a lot, hits monster homers, and is a rock-solid man, both physically and emotionally. Only he doesn't strike out as much as Thome. Chronic elbow problems have prevented him from playing first base full time, but he's a designated hitter. In 2005, he batted .305 with 33 homers, 105 RBI, and a .408 on-base percentage.

Ryan Drese and Einar Diaz for Hafner?

You'd make that trade again.

Coco Crisp became a .300 hitter, a fan favorite with 62 extra base hits.

Chuck Finley for Crisp?

Gotta love that trade.

The Indians signed pitchers Rafael Betancourt, Scott Sauerbeck, Bobby Howry, and Scott Elarton all as free agents. All had a history of arm problems. None cost any real money. All came back to be effective: Elarton won 11 games as a fifth starter; Howry, Sauerbeck, and Betancourt were productive in the bullpen. A big part of dealing in baseball today is signing injured players cheap, then working to rehabilitate them. It doesn't always succeed. The Indians spent time on Juan Gonzalez, Paul Shuey, and Jason Bere in 2005. They didn't come back from their injuries.

Russell Branyan for Ben Broussard?

Another good deal.

While Broussard can be extremely streaky, he's the model of consistency compared to Branyan. Broussard was the Tribe's starting first baseman in 2004 and 2005. He may not be the long-term answer, but he's a viable major league player.

In 2005, Grady Sizemore became a starter at the age of twenty-two. When the Indians were desperate for a leadoff hitter, he moved into the spot in the middle of May and was superb. In his

158 games, he batted .289 with 22 homers, 22 steals, 37 doubles, 11 triples, and 81 RBI. Not even in their most optimistic projections did the Indians believe Sizemore could play so well, so soon.

Cliff Lee went into the rotation in 2004 and won 14 games. In 2005, he was even better, with an 18–5 record, a 3.79 ERA.

Of course, when you deal in baseball, you can fail.

You can have every scout tell you that Brandon Phillips will be a big league star—as the Indians did—but every scout sometimes is wrong. Phillips was a miss, at least in his first three tries to stick with the Tribe. Perhaps that will change, or perhaps he'll be traded. But Phillips had too big a swing and too little plate discipline to be a consistent hitter in the majors. If anything, he regressed as a hitter. No one is sure why. It could have been discouragement. It could have been that he'd never dealt with athletic failure before. It simply could be that he wasn't mature enough.

Looking back, the most important trade of Shapiro's tenure, the one destined to make or break the team's rebuilding process, was Bartolo Colon for Phillips, Lee, and Sizemore.

Colon became a Cy Young Award winner in 2005, a 21-game winner for the Angels. It was the second time he'd won 20 games since being traded by the Indians (he also finished the 2002 season with 20 wins). But the Indians would not have been able to afford to keep Colon, once he became a free agent after 2003. Exchanging him for an 18-game winner in Lee and a future star in Sizemore was a terrific trade, despite the struggles of Phillips. The reason the Indians insisted upon a third prospect in that deal, Sizemore, is because they knew the odds were at least one of the young players wouldn't produce. At the time of the trade, Phillips seemed like the best bet, Sizemore the longest shot. The opposite turned out to be true.

Some of the deals were sidetracked.

Paul Shuey was traded to the Dodgers for Ricardo Rodriguez and Francisco Cruceta. Rodriguez had a sensational spring in 2003 and made the team. He struggled, was injured, and was eventually traded to Texas for Ryan Ludwick, an outfielder with power. Rodriguez was hurt again with Texas, Ludwick kept getting injured with the Tribe. Cruceta failed to make the majors. Shuey had major injuries and retired early in 2005. That trade fizzled for every team involved.

In the end, it was a decent deal for the Tribe only because they dumped Shuey's $3 million contract for 2004.

Before the 2005 season, the Indians signed free-agent third baseman Aaron Boone. He was coming off a serious knee surgery. He didn't play at all in 2004. He made $6.5 million in 2003. The Indians signed him for $4 million. They hoped he'd come back strong, be the type of player who averaged 25 homers and 90 RBI in 2002–2003. He hit .243 with 16 homers and 60 RBI. He played an above-average third base, but was slump prone. While his knee seemed sound, his game was rusty. Heading into 2006, Boone seemed likely to become another third-base stopgap for the Tribe, just as Casey Blake had been before him.

Another free-agent gamble paid off much bigger in 2005.

Shapiro spent much of the winter having his bids for free-agent pitchers turned down. It appeared he'd come up with no one. He was offering $7 million a year, and had no takers. Finally, Kevin Millwood was still available after all the free-agent Christmas shopping was over. He was only thirty and had won 17 games in a season three times. But he had some elbow problems and pitched only 33 innings after the All-Star break. Agent Scott Boras and Shapiro worked out a one-year deal for $7 million. If Millwood missed extended time with elbow problems, he would cost the Indians only $3 million. The risk was on both sides. If Millwood had a big season, he'd be a free agent again and could cash in. If there were more injury problems, the Indians didn't face dire financial consequences. Millwood was spectacular, winning the American League Earned Run Average title with a 2.86 mark. He was only 9–11 because the Indians just didn't score for him.

Indians coaches believed Millwood had a tremendous influence on C.C. Sabathia and Cliff Lee, teaching them how to pitch out of jams, how not to complain when the hitters and defense fail. Here's the kind of year that it was for Millwood: He had a 1.33 ERA in four starts against the World Series–winning White Sox, yet his record was 0–2. He allowed four earned runs in four games, and didn't win any of them. His 2.86 ERA was the lowest by a Tribe starter who pitched at least 162 innings since Dennis Eckersley had a 2.60 ERA in 1975. All of that meant the Indians had absolutely, positively no chance of keeping Millwood after the 2005 season, but that was a given when the experiment began on January 8, 2005, when Millwood agreed to the one-year deal. He was a one-year rent-a-veteran.

But Millwood was the anchor of a rotation with three 15-game winners: Jake Westbrook, Sabathia, and Lee. The bullpen was strong with Bob Wickman coming back from elbow surgery to save 45 games and make the All-Star team.

The Indians finished the season with the lowest ERA (3.61) in the American League, as well as the best bullpen (2.80 ERA).

It seems that every year, Shapiro makes a decision that fans just hate.

Following the 2004 season, it was not picking up the contract option for veteran shortstop and fan favorite Omar Vizquel. Nor did he offer Vizquel a viable deal. And Vizquel originally had a sincere interest in returning to Cleveland until San Francisco offered him a three-year, $12 million contract. At the age of 37, that was a shocker, but Vizquel had a brilliant 2005. He made only eight errors in 152 games and won a Gold Glove in the National League. He batted .271 with 24 steals, three homers, and 45 RBI.

At the end of the 2005 season, fans still missed Vizquel, primarily because he was the last link to the 1990s Jacobs Field glory days. His replacement was Jhonny Peralta, who had been the MVP of the Class AAA International League in 2004. Peralta finished the 2005 season at the ripe old age of twenty-three with a team record for homers (24) by a shortstop. He also had 35 doubles and 78 RBI and batted .292. He was no Vizquel in the field, but adequate.

When you play the stick-to-the-tight-budget game that now rules in the Indians' front office, it makes no sense to keep Vizquel when a prospect such as Peralta is ready.

"If we had a higher payroll, we definitely would have signed Omar," said Shapiro. "We still thought he could play. It wasn't like we wanted to jump off this guy before he drops. But even with a higher payroll, it would have been hard to give him three years, like the Giants did. But knowing we had a limited payroll . . . and knowing we had an alternative . . . granted, not proven, but a real prospect who was MVP of the International League at twenty-two, whom our baseball people really liked . . . the question becomes: Do you bring back Omar for popularity, or do you commit to the young player and use the extra money for pitching? Because if we sign Omar, we don't have the money to get Millwood."

These are the choices that Shapiro and his staff face several times each season. You don't get to pick Vizquel *and* Millwood. It's Millwood *or* Vizquel. You can't just outbid the Red Sox for Matt Clement, who was the Tribe's first off-season free-agent target. You have to sign players like Wickman and Boone coming off injuries, hoping they'll regain something close to their old form. You can sign them because they were hurt, otherwise they'd be too expensive.

Most of all, you have to keep finding prospects. Do it through scouting, drafting, and the farm system, or do it through trades. But keep the young, low-paid talent coming. Fans don't like to hear this, but that's reality for the Indians now—and for more than half of the teams in baseball. The Indians outplayed most other teams in 2005 because they had more and better young players. In 2005, they had no idea Peralta or Sizemore would produce at nearly All-Star levels. But they believed both would eventually become impact players. In the opener, Peralta made a key error against the White Sox. He was pressing early in the season. Manager Eric Wedge even benched Peralta for the home opener, using veteran Alex Cora. Peralta booted several other easy chances early in the year. Victor Martinez was in a horrendous slump for more than two months. Sabathia had six weeks when he could barely survive five innings. The Indians were 9–14 in April, and only 51–49 after the first 100 games.

"In May, we still weren't sure if we'd contend," said Paul Dolan. "I liked the moves that Mark made. I liked our young players. But we were struggling. I started to wonder, what if we didn't contend? Then we'd have to wait another year or two for the next wave of young players to develop. We might have to plug in some journeyman veterans to buy some more time. Hey, doubts do creep in. What if this isn't what we thought it would be? You ask if the plan will fizzle. We had a Plan B and Plan C, but that would take more time—and really, who wanted to go through that? Our best young players were there. Our credibility was at stake."

After Vizquel's departure, a slow start carrying over into a long, mediocre summer would become a public relations disaster. But the young players did come through. In addition to the continued growth of Hafner, Victor Martinez proved that his two minor league batting titles were indications of his becoming an impact player. He's a switch-hitting catcher who has power and can hit for average. In Hafner, Martinez, Peralta, and Sizemore the Indians have four young position players who may become All-Stars.

The Indians still had an imperfect team. They had weaknesses at first (Broussard), third (Boone), and right field (Blake). All three batted in the lower third of the lineup and killed countless rallies. Yet the team still finished 93–69. With typical Tribe luck,

93 wins would have been enough to make the playoffs from the Central Division in nine of the previous eleven years. Some fans say the bottom line was, the Tribe missed the playoffs. But the goal for 2005 had been to contend and to do it with young players who would be around for a while. The Indians did just that.

"The easiest thing to do would have been to keep Robbie Alomar and the other players back in 2002, play it out, and win 85 games," said Shapiro. "The next year [2003], it would have been obvious at some point that we were heading toward a rebuilding process. We may have played close to .500. But by 2004, we would have finally had to rebuild. It would have been clear to everyone. There would have been a normal, gradual decline from deterioration, old players, and a barren farm system. Then we'd be in an eight- to ten-year cycle to try to contend. Pittsburgh has been doing it over and over. So has Cincinnati and Milwaukee, over and over again with new plans."

Shapiro's point is that the moves were about more than just saving money, they were aimed at saving any hope of contention in the next few years.

"For me, 2005 was more a sense of relief than anything else," said Paul Dolan. "If anyone should be gratified, it's Mark. He took us on this course."

While the Dolans remain the most criticized owners in current Cleveland sports, they deserve praise for sticking with their front office. Like Dick Jacobs, they put baseball people in place and let them make the baseball decisions. Then they didn't panic when criticized, and remained supportive of Shapiro.

"Every GM would like a bigger payroll," said Shapiro. "But other than that, I have one of the best working environments in baseball. The Dolans have created that for me. I get freedom to do my job. It's me who is held accountable. I really appreciate that."

CHAPTER 14

THERE'S ALWAYS ONE MORE DEAL

"I DON'T JUST WANT TO HAVE
A GOOD YEAR, I WANT TO GET TO
THE PLAYOFFS EVERY YEAR."

Mark Shapiro knew the fans wouldn't like it.

Not any of it.

They'd still be upset about the collapse in the final week of the 2005 season, costing the Indians a spot in the playoffs. They'd be upset because ownership was not about to make a major increase in the $45 million payroll, at least not to something like $75 million, with which the general manager could go on a free-agent shopping spree. And now teams were calling about Coco Crisp, and Shapiro had to consider trading one of the team's most popular players if the offer became tempting enough.

If the Indians were to stay in contention for the next few years, Shapiro had to keep dealing.

"This job is not a popularity contest," he said. "My own popularity has never been a factor in the moves we've made. Think about what I've been through in the last few years."

Shapiro's first major trade as general manager was after the 2001 season, the Robbie Alomar deal.

Fans didn't like it.

In the middle of the 2002 season, he traded Bartolo Colon.

Fans didn't like it.

After the 2002 season, the Indians lost Jim Thome to Philadelphia via free agency.

Fans didn't like it.

After the 2003 season, he tried to trade Omar Vizquel to Seattle. The deal fell through when the Mariners said Vizquel's surgically repaired knee failed the physical.

Fans didn't like that either, even though the trade was nullified.

After the 2004 season, Vizquel left for San Francisco as a free agent.

Fans really didn't like that.

During this time, the Indians never signed a big-name free agent, and money was just one of the reasons.

Fans never understood that.

"We are always trying to pay players for what they are *going* to do," said Shapiro. "Not for what they have done. That's the core difference between how we look at this and how most fans see it."

To the Indians' front office, a name is just a name. Had they signed Manny Ramirez after the 1999 season or Thome after the 2002 season, they never would have contended in 2005. And they'd be staring at mediocrity for the rest of the decade, begging teams to take those big names and even bigger contracts so the Indians would have room to deal.

After the 2005 season, Shapiro and his staff looked at the 93 victories and realized something: "This was not a season to build from. We want to find a way to win 93 games *again*. In nine of the last eleven years, winning 93 games would have gotten us into the playoffs. If we could sign up for 93 wins every year, we would. In this market with this payroll, 93 wins is an exceptional year. Most teams in baseball are dying to win 93 games."

How could the Indians do that again? And how could they possibly beat out the White Sox, whose payroll was approaching $90 million after winning the World Series? How could the Indians compete with attendance projections for 2006 at only 2.1

million, a modest increase from 2005, and therefore a payroll in the $55 million range?

Shapiro knew he had to keep dealing and that some of the deals would not be popular or understood.

The Indians made this priority list:

1. Sign an established big league starter. It would be nice to think they could retain Kevin Millwood, but no one believed that would happen.

2. Sign a closer to a multiyear deal, if possible.

3. Upgrade the run production by adding a right fielder or a first baseman.

4. Acquire a veteran setup reliever, or a veteran fifth starter if they lost Scott Elarton.

Shapiro stressed to his staff that the Indians were not "looking at just a one-year window, we have several years of contention ahead." This meant he didn't want to take any major risks to win the division in 2006 that would cost him a chance to win in 2007 or later. That's what so many teams do when they start free-agent shopping. They act like it's Christmas Eve and they have to get something *right now*. They give little thought to how it fits or if it will still be worth the price in a few years. It's all about immediate gratification.

The temptation is to look at a player's previous seasons and assume he will perform that way again. Sometimes they do, but often they don't. Or they will for a year or two, but not for the length of an expensive four-year contract. The Indians' key free agent after the 2005 season was Millwood, the American League Earned Run Average leader and the member of the pitching staff most respected by the players, coaches, and management.

As Shapiro said, "He represents everything we want in our players in terms of character."

So why not sign him again?

Shapiro said, "The question we ask on every player is, will we be paying him for what he's done in the past or what he'll do in the future? Most teams make mistakes by simply paying for past production. When you start giving out big contracts, you better be sure the guy can do it in the future."

The reason the Indians were able to sign Millwood to a one-year, $7 million deal in 2005 was because there were questions about his elbow. It had been a problem in 2004. He was absolutely healthy in 2005. But would he continue to hold up? The Indians were willing to talk about a three-year deal worth about $10 million annually.

"That was way out of our comfort zone, but we'd do it because of our enormous respect for the player," said Shapiro.

Shapiro was almost positive his attempts to sign Millwood early would be rejected by agent Scott Boras, who prefers to have his free agents wait while other players sign and the market grows. In this free-agent class, Boras had four starting pitchers: Jarrod Washburn, Jeff Weaver, Kenny Rogers, and Millwood. He rated Millwood as the one most likely to receive the largest free-agent contract given to a pitcher. Three years and $30 million weren't even a beginning point for a discussion with Boras.

Millwood was thirty, and he'd never had more than a two-year contract. In 2005, he had a "platform year," as Shapiro called it, a terrific season putting him in position to cash in. He might never be in this spot again.

So the Indians were looking at other starters. They knew the Boras triangle of Weaver, Washburn, and Rogers would all probably be too expensive. Boras consistently convinces teams to pay more and give out longer contracts than the Indians and most teams could afford.

They did talk to Boras about Rogers, a forty-one-year-old lefty who was 14–8 with a 3.46 ERA for Texas. He also was suspended for shoving a TV cameraman. The Indians mentioned the idea of a Millwood-type deal for Rogers, a one-year contract. Hey, the guy was forty-one. He had some baggage. As Shapiro said, "He seemed to be a distressed property."

Much like Millwood the season before.

But Boras insisted Rogers would get at least two years from some team.

That team would not be the Indians. That team became the Tigers, who paid $17 million over two years for Rogers.

The Indians talked to Matt Morris, who was 14–10 with a 4.11 ERA for St. Louis. They were thinking about a two-year deal, especially since Morris had a 5.32 ERA after the All-Star break. San Francisco paid $27 million over three years for Morris.

In free-agent shopping, there are far more misses than hits. That's especially true if a team plans to shop wisely. It's not just a matter of being cheap, but also being smart—especially when it comes to pitchers, who are injured so often. The Indians were willing to pay $10 million annually for three years to Millwood. They were offering deals in the $7 million range to a few starters, but they wanted the contract kept to two years. The Indians had long appreciated Paul Byrd, a right-handed Jamie Moyer. Most hitters had no idea how he got them out. He didn't throw hard. He had no trick pitch. There was nothing exceptional about him, other than his control.

"There's something else," said *Akron Beacon Journal* baseball writer Sheldon Ocker. "He throws below hitting speed, in the low and middle 80s. That can mess up hitters as much as a guy throwing in the high 90s."

Byrd would be thirty-five on opening day of 2006. He had a history of arm problems and a history of pitching effectively when healthy. But he made 31 starts for the Angels in 2005, pitching into the sixth inning all but three times. His record was 12–11 with a 3.74 ERA. After September 1, and including two postseason starts, Byrd was 3–2 with a 2.25 ERA. The Indians wanted a veteran pitcher with experience in big games to replace

Millwood. The Indians also liked his career 20–6 record against teams in the Tribe's Central Division. Of course, being 5–0 with a 1.60 ERA against the Indians sure helped those numbers. But he was a combined 14–5 against Minnesota, Detroit, and the White Sox.

"He hasn't missed a start for a year and a half," said Chris Antonetti. "He was near the top of the league in quality starts. "

A quality start is pitching at least six innings, allowing three or fewer runs. The Indians love this statistic. Byrd ranked high with twenty-two quality starts. He had turned down a two-year, $12 million offer from the Angels.

"This is a very reliable person who wanted to pitch for us," said Shapiro. "There were issues. He'll be thirty-five all season. He's had arm problems in the past. But the market was giving most starters of his caliber at least three-year deals. We would have been more comfortable with a one-year contract, but we offered two years."

Then Kansas City tried to entice Byrd with a three-year, $21 million deal. But at this stage of his career, Byrd wanted to pitch for a contender. That wasn't Kansas City. For one of the few times in Tribe history, a free agent from another team rejected more money elsewhere to sign with the Indians.

Byrd's contract was $14.25 million for two years.

In the meantime, Boras was cashing in with his starters. In addition to Rogers pocketing $17 million from Detroit, Jarrod Washburn signed with Seattle for a $37 million deal for four years. That's right, $37 million for a guy who was 8–8 with a 3.20 ERA for the Angels in 2005, but only 29–31 over three years. Seattle had originally hoped to sign Millwood to a deal like that, but Boras pushed them in Washburn's direction.

That's because he had another team in mind for Millwood, a team desperate for pitching. It's the team that Boras convinced to pay $258 million for ten years for Alex Rodriguez. A team that periodically tosses around big free-agent money, usually receiving little in return. And Texas gave Millwood $60 million over five years.

After losing Byrd, Kansas City turned to Tribe free agent Scott Elarton, offering him $8 million over two years. The Indians wanted Elarton only on a one-year contract. He was 11–9 with a 4.61 ERA for the Tribe. He is a flyball pitcher with a flat fastball when it's more than a few inches above the knees. That makes him vulnerable to home runs, and he served up 32 in 181 innings. He also has a history of arm problems.

Look at the free-agent market for a moment. Seattle tried to sign Millwood, and ended up with Washburn. The Royals tried to sign Byrd, and ended up with Elarton. The Indians said they were expecting to lose Millwood, content to sign Byrd and prepared to pick a fifth starter from young arms belonging to Jason Davis, Fausto Carmona, and Jeremy Sowers. This was the third season they had been looking for a slot for Davis, and it seemed time to find out if he could cut it as a regular starter.

Then they realized that, in the free-agent gold rush for starters, someone was left alone on the side of the road.

Jason Johnson had an uninspiring 8–13 record with a 4.54 ERA for Detroit in 2005. The Indians' research revealed that the right-hander with a 92 mph fastball and a hard sinker had made at least 32 starts in each of the last three seasons. Remember how they love quality starts? In 2005, Johnson's 19 of 33 starts fell into that category. On the 2005 Tribe, only Jake Westbrook and Millwood had more—both with 20.

"We began to ask ourselves, what were the chances of us having five starters make at least 31 starts, like they did in 2005?" said Shapiro. "The odds are that may never happen again. We decided we didn't need to build a five-man rotation, it needed to be a seven, even an eight-man rotation to cover us in case of injuries. The desire is always to find a rotation of seven to eight starters, because most years you need them. That's why Jason Johnson was appealing to us—especially given the value of what we could sign him for."

In 2005, the Indians used only six starting pitchers. The only other American League team whose rotation stayed that healthy and effective was the White Sox. By contrast, in 2004 and 2003, the Indians used exactly a dozen different starters. The last time they went to the World Series, 1997, they also used a dozen.

"It's hard to find guys who can consistently pitch close to 200 innings in the American League," said Shapiro. "Johnson has done it."

From 2003 to 2005, Johnson threw 190, 197, and 215 innings.

"Getting those kind of innings from a starter is invaluable," said Shapiro.

The problem was that his record in those three years was 26–38 with a 4.62 ERA. He had a pattern of pitching reasonably well before the All-Star break (19–18, 3.98) and poorly after (7–20, 5.43). At thirty-two, it didn't appear Johnson was much more than an "innings eater," hardly an endearing or exciting term. If he happened to be a boxer, it would mean he could take a punch. In this case, it means he kept pitching. Not always well, but he pitched. In the last three years, opposing batters hit .283 against him.

From 2003 to 2005, Johnson made 98 starts. In the American League, only Barry Zito (104), Mark Buehrle (103), Bartolo Colon (101), and Mike Maroth (100) had more. The Indians liked how he had the second-best ground ball/fly ball ratio in the American League, behind only the Tribe's Jake Westbrook. His sinker is the reason.

"He has a phenomenal work ethic," said Antonetti. "We think that he overtrains, and that's why he has worn down by the end of the last few seasons. He's durable, he has good character, and we think he can improve with us."

He also has diabetes, but that supposedly is under control.

Most of all, he was affordable. Other teams did not value innings quite as much as Shapiro. Johnson was anxious to get out of Detroit and sincerely wanted to pitch for the Tribe, where he had watched Elarton and others revive their careers.

"We had a chance to sign a guy who pitched 200 innings to a one-year deal under $4 million—that's a good use of money in this free-agent market," said Shapiro. "He gives us a chance to offset the loss of Elarton and maybe even improve on Elarton's performance. I wanted depth because I know that in most seasons, at some point, your third starter becomes your second starter. And your fourth starter becomes your third. And so on. I like the idea of have five experienced starting pitchers with your kids behind them."

They signed Johnson to a one-year deal worth $3.5 million, although he can make another $2 million if he starts 33 games and pitches at least 215 innings. For the Indians, this seems like a smart buy. If he pitches well, he'll be a bargain. If he flops, they only have to pay him for one year.

"What changed almost immediately after I took the job was the emphasis on flexibility," said Shapiro. "You don't want to give out many long-term deals. Generally, the shorter the contract, the better unless it's a player you know very, very well."

But Shapiro did want a closer for more than one year. He'd never say it, but there were concerns about Bob Wickman. Wickman found a way to save 45 games while allowing 79 base runners and nine homers in 62 innings. He only struck out 45. In three years, runners were 21 of 21 in stealing bases. But he was 45 of 50 in saves. He did it by holding opposing hitters to a .149 average with runners on base, the lowest of any American League reliever. Wickman would hunt for three outs, walking some hitters, sometimes loading the bases. Opposing hitters were only 2 of 26 against Wickman with two outs and runners in scoring position. On opening day of 2006, he was thirty-seven, battling his weight, and had struggled with arm problems as recently as 2004.

The question was if he could do it again. Or would he fade?

Yet Wickman finished 2005 strong, saving 29 of 30 games and allowing only one run in his last 16 appearances.

Shapiro believed that Wickman would still be available later in the winter, so he looked at other closers. The Indians were one of the first teams to interview free agent B.J. Ryan. They made a three-year offer in the $20 million range. They considered raising it to $28 million over four years. But Toronto overwhelmed everyone (including Ryan) by signing him to a five-year, $47 million deal. Most Major League Baseball executives thought the Blue Jays had gone totally insane. Ryan had a dominating season with a 2.43 ERA and 100 strikeouts in 70 innings. He was 36 of 41 in saves.

But there should be this rule in baseball: You can't sign a player to a contract worth more millions than the guy has career saves. In this case, Ryan ended 2005 with 42 lifetimes saves, yet his deal was $47 million.

Shapiro's next stop was San Diego, where he pursued Trevor Hoffman. He would be thirty-eight on opening day. His best pitch is a changeup. He was 43 of 46 in saves. He had a 2.97 ERA, striking out 54 in 58 innings. He had spent the last twelve years with the Padres and lived in San Diego. As one Padres executive said, "Notice when the Indians talked to him this winter, they didn't fly him to Cleveland. They went to San Diego."

Shapiro and Wedge did their best possible selling job, and Hoffman was sincerely interested for a while. But in the end, he was not about to leave home, which was San Diego. The Padres signed him to a two-year, $13 million deal. The Indians were offering a little more for two years with incentives built in so that a third year would be guaranteed at $8 million. It's surprising the

Indians pursued Hoffman that hard and were willing to guarantee a deal that would carry him to age forty. It seemed a bigger risk than normal for the Tribe, but Shapiro was especially impressed by Hoffman. The same was true of Brian Giles, the former Tribe outfielder who was a free agent with the Padres. He was at the top of the Tribe's list of position players, and they were willing to offer Giles at least $30 million over three years. He signed for slightly less to stay with the Padres.

"Both guys made values-based decisions," said Shapiro. "I respect that. It's that part of their character that made them so appealing to us. We offered them both more than they took to stay with the Padres."

The Indians checked out Tom Gordon, but the Phillies signed him to a three-year, $18 million deal. He would be thirty-eight on opening day and has been an inconsistent closer, but a solid setup man. The Indians believed Gordon was outlandishly overpriced.

That's because Shapiro and his staff have developed this theory about relief pitchers: *You just don't know.*

That's it—*you just don't know.*

In most cases, you just don't know how they will pitch from one season to the next. The Indians believe relievers are the most inconsistent performers of any players, any position. There are exceptions, such as Mariano Rivera and Hoffman, but not many.

"I want no credit for building the best bullpen in the American League [in 2005]," Shapiro said. "Luck was a part of it. Look at Texas. In 2004, they had the American League's best bullpen. In 2005, they probably were the worst. The Braves are great with pitchers, and they don't have a formula for having a consistent bullpen. More mistakes are made by signing relievers to big contracts . . ."

Shapiro stopped, and then gave his reasons:

1. You don't see them as much as other players. A regular posi-

tion player has more than 500 at-bats. A starting pitcher throws at least 180 innings. Very few relievers pitch more than 70 innings. In 2005, Wickman pitched 62 innings.

2. The better a reliever pitches, the more often he pitches. Bob Howry was a hot setup man for the Tribe in 2005, and he appeared in 79 games, which was a team record for the Tribe. It was the third most in the American League. This can lead to over-work. "That's why you see a guy having a great season one year, then a bad one the next," said Shapiro. "Then he doesn't pitch as much because he's having a bad year—and the next year, he pitches well because he rested his arm the year before. Some of the best buys are guys coming off bad years because they hadn't pitched that much and their arms are rested."

3. Relievers are relievers for a reason. They usually don't have as many pitches as a good starter. They also may have more weak-nesses. Their edge is slight, and that's why fatigue or even a minor injury can make a major impact.

4. The mental game is hard to judge. Some pitchers can't han-dle the pressure of closing, but they pitch well in the eighth in-ning. Some are effective when their team is behind, but struggle when asked to hold a lead at almost any point in the game. "One of the things I love about Wickman is he knows how to handle the blown save," said Shapiro. "Not many can do that."

5. Relievers can come out of nowhere . . . and then go back to nowhere. Shapiro talked about Bobby Jenks, who finished the 2005 season as closer for the World Champion White Sox. He was the same Bobby Jenks who was put on waivers by the Angels after the 2004 season. He was coming off arm problems. He'd never pitched an inning in the majors. He had always been a starter in the minors. His minor league record was 18–29 with a 4.95 ERA. The White Sox claimed him for $20,000. He was the third closer they used in 2005. They began with Shingo Takatsu, a Japanese import who faded. Next, it was Dustin Hermanson, who was ef-

fective until his back started bothering him. Jenks opened the 2005 season in Class AA, then closed in the World Series.

6. Jose Mesa came to the Indians as a hard-throwing, under-achieving starter in 1992. He was moved to the bullpen in 1994, set a team record with 46 saves in 1995, and flamed out in Game 7 of the 1997 World Series. By 1998, he'd lost the closer's job and was traded to San Francisco. In 1999, he saved 33 games for Se-attle, but lost the closer's job in 2000. In 2001, he saved 42 games for the Phillies, and has been up and down ever since. Mesa's story is a bit extreme, but the inconsistency among relievers is quite common.

Shapiro didn't say it, but these reasons are a safe guess why the Indians didn't fight hard to keep Howry as a free agent. They wanted Howry, but the Cubs offered a three-year, $12 million deal. He does have a history of arm problems. He had elbow surgery in 2003, was cut by Boston, and signed by the Indians. Howry opened the 2004 season in the minors, then came to the Tribe on June 29, 2004. He has been strong ever since. Will he continue to be one of the best setup men in baseball, or is he headed for an off year, as is so common when relievers pitch as much as Howry did in 2005? The Indians didn't want to gamble three years to find out.

The Indians considered Todd Jones, but the Tigers signed the sometime closer to a two-year, $11 million contract. Jones was thirty-eight on April 24, 2006. His record is even more erratic than that of Mesa. The Indians thought about him on a one-year deal, but Detroit gave Jones nearly the same contract it handed to Troy Percival before the 2005 season. The Indians liked Percival for one year in the $5 million range. Detroit gave him $12 million over two seasons. The thirty-five-year-old lasted 25 innings, was injured, missed the rest of the 2005 season, then retired.

So the Indians went to Wickman with a one-year, $5 million deal. He signed it. There were a few other teams mildly interested, but Wickman preferred to return where he believed the team would contend and he'd close.

"He wasn't happy about us talking to other guys," said Shapiro. "But I'm not about to apologize for paying him $5 million. We had a very candid discussion about his situation. I think he'll have an edge to him, and that could be good. He'll want to show what he can do."

During the winter, something else was happening. Coco Crisp had become a hot item.

Atlanta and Boston wanted Crisp. The Indians had some preliminary talks with the Braves about a minor league third baseman named Andy Marte. Tribe scouts loved him. The two teams couldn't put together a package. Boston was desperate for Crisp to play center field, replacing Johnny Damon, who had signed with the Yankees as a free agent. Crisp was appealing to many teams in need of a center fielder. He has excellent speed. He doesn't draw a lot of walks, but hits .300 and plays with a spark. The Indians had Grady Sizemore in center and expected him to be there for years. Shapiro kept telling Boston that he wasn't interested. He had no one to replace Crisp in left field. And what Boston offered was of little interest.

Then the Red Sox traded with Atlanta for Marte, sending Edgar Renteria to the Braves. Atlanta was as hungry for a shortstop as the Red Sox were for a center fielder. The Braves had lost Rafael Furcal to the Dodgers via a $39 million free-agent contract. The Braves liked Renteria, despite his subpar year in Boston. In the National League, Renteria was a .287 hitter with two Gold Gloves. Boston not only traded Renteria for Marte, the Red Sox agreed to pay nearly half of the remaining $32 million for the three years left on Renteria's contract. Shapiro said he doubted Boston made that trade simply to acquire Marte and move him to the Indians. But it wasn't a secret that the Indians liked and wanted to deal for Marte. Boston knew there would be no trade for Crisp with its current roster. So the Red Sox traded for the player the Indians wanted. They also are in such a lucrative market, they could pay the Braves to make sure the trade happened, positioning themselves to make a charge for Crisp. At the worst, Boston would end up with a guy who was ranked as the number nine prospect in the game by *Baseball America*. At twenty-one, Marte hit .275 with 20 homers and 74 RBI in Class AAA. He had a .372 on-base percentage combined with a .502 slugging percentage for an impressive OPS of .874.

The Indians liked Marte for theses reasons:

1. The numbers he posted in Class AAA at the age of twenty-one—when most players were still in college or in Class A—showed he was not only major league ready, he can improve at the big league level because he's so young.

2. In each of his four seasons in the minors, he was voted the best defensive third basemen in the league by opposing managers and coaches.

3. Their scouts consistently rated him as a "middle of the order impact hitter with power to all fields." His attitude also was rated "a plus," as was his work ethic.

4. The Indians had no third base prospects in the upper levels of their minor league system.

5. Their current third baseman, Aaron Boone, was thirty-two and coming off a disappointing year. The Indians had signed him despite his missing all of 2004 with knee surgery, because they weren't happy with Casey Blake's defense at third and they had no one else. Boone would serve for a few years until they could find a young third baseman. But they had no viable candidates.

"I felt no pressure or urgency to trade Coco," said Shapiro. "There was no way we'd trade him straight up for Marte, despite how much we liked Marte. There had to be more in the deal, and we had to find a replacement in left field."

But the Indians had a real possibility for left field.

Philadelphia had been calling for months about Arthur Rhodes, a veteran lefty reliever who had a strong first half of the 2005 season for the Tribe but missed most of the last two months because one of his children had a life-threatening illness. He also was bothered by tendinitis of the knee. Rhodes was thirty-six, due to make $3.6 million, and has had the typical roller-coaster career of most veteran relievers. His stats were very good on the surface: 3–1, 2.08 ERA. But it was a concern that Rhodes's main job was to get out lefties, and they batted .286 off him. Righties were only .155.

"He's a veteran and I like him," said Shapiro. "After losing Howry, I wanted to keep him."

The Indians also thought he could have another solid year in 2006, partly because he had pitched so little in 2005. In other words, he wasn't worn out. But the Indians liked an outfielder named Jason Michaels, who had been a reserve with the Phillies for a few years. He would have been the ideal backup outfielder for the Tribe in 2005 because he's something many of their hitters were not—disciplined.

How often did fans moan as Casey Blake, Ben Broussard, and Aaron Boone swung at bad pitches and found themselves hitting from behind in the count? The Indians really like players with a high on-base percentage, at least .340. Here were the numbers for the bottom three of the order: Blake (.308), Boone (.299), and Broussard (.307). The bench was even worse, as utility man Jose Hernandez had a .277 on-base percentage. The one criticism of Crisp as a hitter has been his lack of walks: he had only 44 in 594 at-bats for an on-base percentage of .345 in 2005.

Chris Antonetti studies the statistics of every player in baseball and had been looking for a veteran hitter who could help the Indians by getting on base, working the count, being what John Hart used to call "a professional hitter." When Hart would say that, some of us in the press box would joke, "And what are these other guys making $3 million a year—a bunch of amateurs?" (Though watching some of them at times made you wonder.)

Michaels had platooned in center field for the Phillies, splitting time with former Indian Kenny Lofton. The Indians liked his numbers: a .399 on-base percentage, a .323 batting average versus lefties, and a .336 average in the number two spot of the order, which is where he'd bat if the Indians traded Crisp and acquired him. Shapiro talked to Eric Wedge about Michaels, and Wedge had a vivid memory of Michaels from their days in the International League, when Wedge managed in Buffalo and Michaels was with Scranton: "He plays hard all the time," said the Tribe manager. "I like him. He'd help us."

During the several weeks of trade discussions that eventually led to the Crisp deal, Cincinnati was offering Sean Casey around. The Reds wanted to dump his $8.5 million contract. They were even willing to pay $1.5 million of it. Casey is one of Shapiro's all-time favorite people. They talk each month, have done so for years dating back to Casey's days in the Tribe farm system. While Shapiro understood why Hart traded Casey to Cincinnati for veteran starter Dave Burba—the Indians were desperate for pitching—it pained Shapiro to lose Casey. He consistently hit over .300. In 2005, he batted .312 with nine homers, 58 RBI and a .371 on base percentage. There was some concern about the lack of power from Casey, who played in one of the easiest parks to hit home runs. But in 2004, he batted .324 with 25 homers and 99 RBI. He was thirty-one and perhaps a bit bogged down with all the losing and cost-cutting in Cincinnati. Shapiro decided not to pursue Casey, a disciplined hitter who would have been a definite upgrade at first over Broussard. Casey eventually was traded to the Pirates.

Shapiro would never say this publicly, but if the Indians had a budget in the $75 million to $80 million range, he would have brought in Casey. The first baseman had only one year left on his contract. But not with a budget in the $55 million to $60 million range. It hurt Shapiro to pass on Casey, but he did.

Michaels brought some of the same qualities as Casey in terms of on-base production, only he's a right-handed hitter and an outfielder—which the Indians needed more than a lefty-hitting first baseman such as Casey. The Indians had tried to sign Nomar Garciaparra, with the idea of turning the former shortstop into a right-handed hitting outfielder. But he signed with the Dodgers. No Giles. No Casey. No Garciaparra. No upgrade on the offense at first or the outfield, which was one of Shapiro's goals. He did add veteran first baseman Eduardo Perez to platoon with Broussard at first base. Perez replaced the disappointing Jose Hernandez and signed the same $1.7 million deal Hernandez had in 2005. Perez had hit .255 with 11 homers and 28 RBI in limited action. The hope was that a platoon of Perez and Broussard could produce close to 25 homers and 90 RBI in 2006. Shapiro grew up in Baltimore and admired how former Orioles manager Earl Weaver combined journeyman veteran players, such as Gary Roenicke and John Lowenstein, into a platoon that would yield very productive numbers.

Michaels would be a real asset, either as a regular or a fourth outfielder.

"The only risk was if he could be a regular," said Antonetti. "He'd play at thirty in 2006. He was stuck behind Bobby Abreu and Pat Burrell, two big-time guys making a lot of money, but when Michaels has played, he's been productive and consistent."

Entering 2006, he was a career .310 hitter vs. lefties, .277 vs. righties, and .291 overall. He was making $1.5 million. One area of concern was that Michaels had an altercation with a policeman and was charged with aggravated assault and resisting arrest. The case resulted in no jail time but a hundred hours of community service. Once Michaels completed that, it would be erased from his record. That soft penalty told the Indians there were some mitigating circumstances to the case, as assaulting a policeman usually brings a much stiffer penalty.

"We talked to his lawyers, to the team's lawyers, and we went over the police reports," said Shapiro. "He made a mistake, but we don't think this will be a concern in the future. It was an isolated incident. Our reports say he's a good guy and an excellent teammate."

For weeks before the Crisp deal, the Phillies were willing to trade Michaels for Rhodes. It seemed Shapiro should have just made the deal, regardless of what happened with Boston. But he was worried about his bullpen, so he hesitated.

The Indians continued to talk to Boston—about forty different proposals went between the two teams. The Indians wanted another prime prospect besides Marte. The Indians pushed hard for Manny Delcarmen, a twenty-four-year-old righty reliever with a 95 mph fastball who had a 3–1 record with a 2.45 ERA and 49 strikeouts in 390 innings in Class AAA. Late in the season, he allowed three runs in nine impressive innings with Boston. The Red Sox believed it was almost impossible to trade Delcarmen— not just because of his obvious talent, but also because he's a Boston native. They just didn't want to deal with their fans on that issue—they had been rooting for their native son for years in the team's farm system.

The Indians convinced Boston to put catching prospect Kelly Shoppach into the deal. The Indians were willing to toss backup catcher Josh Bard into the package. Wedge had lost confidence in him, and rarely used Bard. The same was true of reliever David Riske. Wedge did not like to pitch Riske in a tie game or when ahead. There were concerns he was losing velocity from his fastball. Boston put veteran reliever Guillermo Mota into the trade.

The deal would be done when Mota passed a physical, but then everything nearly fell apart. The Phillies suddenly had another trading partner for Michaels. Without the Rhodes/Michaels trade first, Shapiro would not send Crisp, along with Riske and Bard, to Boston for Marte, Shoppach, and Mota.

Mota's physical for his arm revealed some concerns. The elbow may hold up, or not. He had not pitched well in September (8.22 ERA in 7.2 innings). Overall, he was 2–2 with a 4.70 ERA and did pitch 67 innings. He had been one of the game's best setup men in 2003 and part of 2004, but has struggled since. Shapiro had hoped Mota could replace Rhodes as a veteran in the seventh or eighth inning. Suddenly, he wasn't sure.

Boston remained fixed on Crisp. Shapiro pushed for another prospect instead of Mota. Boston had another idea—money. Mota would make $3 million. What if Boston assumed nearly all the risk for Mota? The Red Sox agreed to pay $2.3 million, meaning the Indians would get Mota for a mere $700,000. Shapiro asked for more. What if Mota was hurt for most of the year? Boston said it would toss in another $1.7 million or give the Indians a chance to pick from a list of prospects in their system.

As the new Boston offer was coming together, Philadelphia called. The Rhodes/Michaels deal had to be done now or the Phillies were going to a different team. They had to know. Shapiro made the trade for Michaels. That freed him to trade Crisp.

The Indians were bringing in veteran relievers Steve Karsay and Danny Graves as reclamation projects. It was much like they'd done recently with Howry, Betancourt, and others. Not all come back, but some do. Shapiro figured that among Mota, Graves, and Karsay, one of them is likely to make a comeback, perhaps even two. Karsay and Graves signed minor league contracts, so they were the perfect frugal gambles. The more he thought about it, the more he realized he could live without Rhodes.

Some fans have said the trade was about money. That's true only to the extent that nearly every baseball trade is about money. Boston has tons of it. The Red Sox were willing to pay more than

$15 million on Renteria's contract to obtain Marte. Now they were able to toss in $2.3 million on Mota. They were eating more than $17 million in contracts, yet feeling absolutely no financial heartburn. A team with one of baseball's most lucrative cable TV contracts could do that.

Shapiro did some math. He would save about $2 million on the Rhodes/Michaels deal. Crisp was in line for a $2.5 million contract. He also was tossing in Bard and Riske, who'd make about $2.5 million combined in 2006. He'd pick up about $1.5 million in contracts from Boston. He was saving about $4 million.

The $4 million was important because it gave him money to spend later in 2006 on other deals.

Shapiro was sold on Marte as exactly what the scouts said—a future run-producing third baseman. He liked Shoppach, who was a strong defensive catcher who threw out 44 percent of stealing base runners in Class AAA in 2005. In the previous two Class AAA seasons, Shoppach hit 48 homers. His batting average was only .243 in those years combined, but a catcher with a powerful arm and a bat with some punch is a valuable commodity. He could either back up Martinez, or be used in a future trade.

In the end, Shapiro made the trade because he didn't see any other way he could get a major-league-ready third-base prospect like Marte.

Shapiro knew the fans would be unhappy and most of the media wouldn't understand his latest deal, but in the end, he couldn't worry about that. They hadn't liked most of his moves. Being right was more important than being popular.

"I don't want to be Executive of the Year in January," Shapiro said. "That usually is the guy who spends the most money, and most of the time, all those free-agent signings don't work out because you ended up overpaying."

Owners Paul and Larry Dolan were strongly behind Shapiro

on the trade, although they were willing to support him if he decided to back out of the deal. As owners, they have never been given enough credit for allowing their young management team to make risky, unpopular moves and take the public relations heat. They've allowed Shapiro to build his own organization, and they stay out of meddling with the baseball side.

"I know that I have a very unique situation," Shapiro. "Very few executives have as much freedom and support as I do from their owners."

In many ways, the Indians are operating like the Oakland A's, who continue to stay in contention despite making big deals involving their biggest-name players. In three days (November 16–18, 2004), A's general manager Billy Beane traded star pitchers Tim Hudson and Mark Mulder primarily for prospects. Mulder was 17–8 with a 4.43 ERA in 2004, Hudson was 12–6 with a 3.53 ERA. Players such as Jason Giambi, Jermaine Dye, Miguel Tejada, and closer Keith Foulke have passed through Oakland. Not all of Beane's moves have been home runs, but his batting average is excellent, as the low-paying A's have won at least 91 games in 2000–2004, and they were 88–74 in 2005.

The idea is to acquire prospects such as Marte, or role players with intriguing statistics like Michaels, and see if they can produce as regulars.

When Tribe fans heard about the Crisp trade, the majority hated it. They named every lousy trade from the last thirty years that brought prospects who fizzled for the Tribe. They forgot the recent deals for Lee, Hafner, Sizemore, and even Crisp. Instead they asked, what about Brandon Phillips? How come he's been stuck in the minors?

"We understand the primary thing fans care about is winning," said Shapiro. "We know the short-term reaction to our trades and moves can be very emotional and negative—even if the national analysts and media like our moves or if *Baseball America* says we got the right prospects. In terms of drawing fans, all that matters is winning. I will go to my grave believing that winning draws more than having a popular player, but a losing team. Most fans don't care if it's a good guy or a bad guy, they just want guys who win. But our core belief as an organization is we want people with good character because they help you win. It's a big part of what we stand for, we not only want to talk that talk, but walk that walk."

For the Indians, it won't get any easier. At some point, the Dolans will have to pick a time when they will indeed spend more than they are projected to take in. It doesn't have to be a wild spree, such as the $96 million payroll they had in 2001. But it's very hard even for the best organizations to consistently win when they are in the bottom 20 percent in payroll, as the Indians were in 2005 and were projected to be again on 2006. Even in 2005, the count-your-quarters A's spent $55 million, about $10 million more than the Tribe. Projections for 2006 had the Indians drawing 2.1 million fans with a payroll in the $55 million range, which would still put them in the bottom 25 percent of baseball. Shapiro and most of his key people are under contract through 2007. They love working for the Indians and with the Dolans, but they also want to win. There will come a time when Shapiro will need ownership to dig a little deeper into their wallets to keep a good thing going.

As Shapiro said, "I don't just want to have a good year, I want to get to the playoffs every year. I want us in position to win 90 or more games every year so we can contend for a title. That's really what my job is all about, consistently putting a winner on the field."

And drastic, daring dealing is the only way for a team like the Indians to do it.

ACKNOWLEDGMENTS

The Cleveland Indians were amazingly open and candid with me for this project. They had no final approval of the manuscript, no control over what I'd write. But they gave countless hours of interviews and lots of material for this book. Those who were especially helpful were Paul Dolan, Mark Shapiro, Chris Antonetti, Ken Stefanov, Bob DiBiasio, Bart Swain, and Tom Hamilton.

Geoff Beckman and Roger Grecni provided research and fact-checking that saved me from countless mistakes; any errors that did slip through are mine.

The *Akron Beacon Journal* has long supported my career as an author. A special thanks goes to Jim Crutchfield, Debra Adams Simmons, and Larry Pantages, who have created a tremendous working environment for me, and also to Mary Lou Woodcock, Sue Reynolds, and Maribeth Lieberth. Thanks to Stephanie Storm for reviewing the text.

I thank God every day for publisher David Gray and my agent, Faith Hamlin. Both know how to make terrific deals that help this author.

Chris Andrikanich and Jane Lassar at Gray & Company have been a great support to me. Every author should be so blessed.

Large parts of this books were written at the Walker Homestead in Hill City, South Dakota, and in Cedar Key, Florida. Thanks to Kim Benning (Heart of the Hills Vacation Homes) and Janet Blackwell (Seahorse Landing).

And no one has been a bigger supporter than Roberta, my wife of 28 years.